ULTRALIGHT
BACKPACKIN' TIPS

HOARY
MARMOT

(*Marmota caligata*)

a practical & philosophical guide (with cartoons)

ULTRALIGHT
BACKPACKIN' TIPS

153 amazing & inexpensive tips for extremely lightweight camping

YEAH BABY!

written & illustrated by
Mike Clelland!

FALCONGUIDES

GUILFORD, CONNECTICUT
HELENA, MONTANA

AN IMPRINT OF ROWMAN & LITTLEFIELD

FALCONGUIDES®

Copyright © 2011 by Mike Clelland!

FalconGuides is an imprint of Rowman & Littlefield
Falcon, FalconGuides, and Outfit Your Mind are registered trademarks of Rowman & Littlefield

Distributed by
NATIONAL BOOK NETWORK

Library of Congress Cataloging-in-Publication Data is available on file.

ISBN 978-0-7627-6384-9

Printed in the United States of America

Contents

Feet

Camping Tips

Sleeping as a Skill

Water

Soggy Conditions

Desert Travel

Bears

Acknowledgments

My thanks to Andrew Skurka, Sheila Baynes, Ryan Jordan, Scott Christy, Ryan Hutchins-Cabibi, Phil Schneider-Pants, Alexa Callison-Burch, Sunny Busby, Sam Haraldson, Allen O'Bannon, Jamie Hunt, Mike Martin, Don Ladigin, Glen Van Peski, and Natascha Jatzeck.

The term ultralight backpacking has a very specific meaning.

It defines the base weight of a fully loaded backpack at the start of a trip.

When you subtract the weight of the consumable items inside the pack

(food, water & fuel),

the remaining weight *must be under ten pounds* to be called ultralight!

These first ten tips are a Manifesto, a proclamation of intent! Everything else in this book can be derived from these very simple ingredients.

The intended goal of this book is to provide some clever insights on how to travel efficiently in the mountains with a *very* light backpack. The hush-hush secret to ultralight backpacking is that it's actually pretty easy, especially solving all the gear issues. The bigger challenge is embracing a new mind-set, and (hopefully) this book will balance these essential factors.

Focus on these initial ten points, and everything else will fall into place.

1.   Get a scale

This is rule number one, and it's absolutely essential. Do not proceed until this is solved. There is simply no way around it; weighing your gear is a prerequisite.

If you are an aspiring ultralight camper, this is the one and only tool that is truly required to get your pack weight to plummet. A simple digital postal scale has accuracy down to a tenth of an ounce, and knowing the weight of every single item is essential.

These are cheap and easy to find; a simple 5-pound digital postal scale from any office supply store is perfect. No need to pay more than 35 bucks, and there are good scales for as little as $19.95.

2.   Comfortable and safe are vital!

Anyone can go out into the mountains with a tiny amount of gear and suffer—it's easy to be cold, hungry, and ill prepared. You need to be warm at night, dry in the rain, well fed, and ready to deal with safety issues. Ultralight camping should be delightful, not stressful. The challenge is to succeed with only the gear that's absolutely needed (see tip 28).

The first-aid kit is a good metaphor for your lightweight camping mind-set. You would be foolish to travel without one, right? But what is *truly* required? What can you effectively improvise? There is a blurry line between TOO heavy and TOO light. You can still go out into the backcountry with a very light pack and be comfortable and safe (see tip 55).

3.   Scrutinize everything!

This entire book could get boiled down to those two words. Do NOT simply put stuff in your pack. Look at every single item, weigh it, document it, hold it in your hand, ponder it, brood on it, and meditate over it. Only after this mindful deliberation should you decide if this item comes along. This cautious

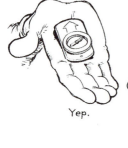

thought process happens for every single item! Do this every time you prep for an outing.

Questions to ask: Will I be fine without this? Is there a lighter option? Can this item serve more than one purpose; is it multiuse? Can I use something else and get the same results? A tent stake can hold your shelter down in the wind and also makes a pretty good trowel for digging a cat-hole, making it a true a multiuse option.

Be extremely meticulous with every decision—and every item. Weigh it, trim it down, and weigh it again.

You either need it or you don't. If you don't need it—it doesn't go in the pack.

Yep.　　Nope.

excellent
ULTRALIGHT
RESOURCE

4.　Make your own stuff, and making it out of trash is always best!

It's super fun to tinker with homemade designs and then put them to use in the backcountry. And quite often the lightest and simplest gear can be salvaged from the trash. The humble plastic water bottle is as light as it gets, and it's essentially free (see tip 102). And an aluminum cat food can pulled out of the garbage makes a very efficient ultralight alcohol stove (see tip 120).

There is a myth that ultralight camping is an expensive undertaking, but it just ain't true (see tip 30). Sure there are a few items where it's nice to purchase a high-quality piece of gear—titanium cookware is wonderfully light, but it comes at a high price. Would an old beer can with the top cut off serve the same purpose?

5.　It's okay to be nerdy

nerd.

I am living proof of this credo. I delight in the quirky problem solving required when wrestling with all the minutia of my pack weight. I encourage you to dig deep and fully accept your inner nerd. It's okay to obsess about half an ounce. I encourage that attitude! I enjoy using my finely crafted do-it-yourself gear in the mountains.

I fully recognize how dorky all this can be, and I acknowledge that I fit every stereotype of the weirdo zealot. But it's fun, and fun counts for a lot. I take great pride wearing my homemade rain skirt in among a team of burly men!

6. Try something new every time you go camping

Don't be content with achieving a homeostasis; you should unceasingly be evolving toward a goal of greater efficiency, comfort, and lighter weight. There will always be some new and interesting thing or technique you can test. Challenge yourself with every outing. If you try something and it doesn't work quite as well as you hoped—*so what!* You learned something valuable by trying. Always try something new, *ALWAYS!*

7. Simply take less stuff!

The easiest way to get an item's weight down to zero is simply NOT to put it in the pack. Yes, this means leaving stuff behind. This is harder than you think. There may be an item (or a bunch of them) that you have simply *always* carried with you, and it might be an ingrained routine to just toss that thing in your pack. Be very self-aware whenever this happens. Question your mind-set: Are you clinging to old habits?

Go through every item you might want to bring and truly ask yourself: *Will I be okay without this thing?*

This answer should be either YES or NO—never maybe.

8. Know the difference between wants and needs

You actually *NEED* very little. Food, water, and oxygen are obvious. So are warmth, comfort, and peace of mind. But we are all too easily swayed by our *WANTS*, especially me!

Some things, like the backpack, are obviously required. But what about the tent? Is that something you WANT or NEED? These are decidedly different, and it can be a challenging human exercise to attempt to separate them from each other. Can you replace the thing you WANT with a something you truly NEED? Is there an option that's lighter, cheaper, simpler, or multiuse? Can it be nixed entirely? It should be easy to ditch the tent and replace it with a tarp, but all too often this decision can be fraught with emotion.

I have a beautiful camping knife. I love this elegantly crafted tool. I feel a very real WANT associated with my well-designed (and expensive) toy. This is a good item to truly scrutinize with ultralight eyes.

Are you hypnotized into believing you NEED a knife when all you really do is WANT a knife? (See tip 53.)

Personally I've found that a 0.1-ounce single-edge razor blade, void of frills and charisma, solves my need for a sharp thing in the mountains. Thus the beautiful knife stays at home, and that liberation feels good!

---

9.   Cut stuff off your gear

the useless LITTLE PLASTIC RING

The ring lives here

STANDARD PLASTIC SODA BOTTLE

The quintessential plastic soda bottle has a lid, and under that lid is a little plastic ring. That extra piece of plastic went on in the factory, and it serves no purpose after you first open the bottle. Use a tiny pair of wire cutters (or your fingernails) and get that thing off. The paltry weight is obviously insignificant in the grand scheme of things. But to me it's more of a mind-set. If you dedicate yourself to these (seemingly) inconsequential items, you are setting yourself up with a heightened level of overall standards. This mind-set will trickle up and influence the big stuff too.

Get a pair of scissors and trim off anything you can, and then reweigh things. The act of shaving off small extraneous stuff will really reinforce your goal. Your backpack, no matter the make or model, can always use a little trimming (see tip 62). Get a razor blade, and go to town on it!

10.   Document your gear

One system involves a three-ring binder and a pencil, and every piece of camping gear gets weighed and noted. The other involves a computerized spreadsheet (see tip 19).

Yes, everything gets weighed on a scale, and all these numbers get written down. This may sound totally nerdy, but this deliberate act makes it very easy to take only what's really needed. And while you're at it, go ahead and write the weight right on each piece of gear with a Sharpie.

The simple act of weighing your gear creates a resolve and focus that'll force you to really think about every piece of gear. Record the totals, and make sure to add a column titled "Why" for each item. If you can't answer "why" you need something— don't take it!

new school

OLD School

11.   Know the lingo

Following is a very short glossary of terms used throughout this book.

Traditional (also **Trad**): Base weight over 20 pounds; usually this means a pack weight of over 35 pounds.

Lightweight: Base weight below 20 pounds. This is totally realistic with just minimal dedication.

TRADITIONAL
BACKPACKER

ULTRALIGHT
BACKPACKER

Ultralight (or **UL**): The term *ultralight* has acquired a very specific meaning in the realm of the nerdy lightweight camping community. It means having a base weight of UNDER 10 pounds. That means everything in your pack that isn't a consumable and isn't worn on your body while hiking totals less than 10 pounds. This may sound daunting, but it can be done with a minimum of dedication. There are a series of skills required for success (all of 'em are in this book), but it's more of a mind-set than a skill set.

Sub-ultralight (or **SUL**): Base weight below 5 pounds! The domain of passionate zealots, it's achievable with a few key items and a more focused mind-set. (See tip 39.)

The Big Three: These are the three heaviest items (or systems) you'll carry: the backpack, sleeping system, and shelter system. (See tip 15.)

PPPPD: An acronym for Pounds Per Person Per Day. This gets used in food calculations. A similar acronym is noted as PPPD, meaning Per Person Per Day. This is a shorthand tool for figuring fuel and rationing.

Multiuse: Some gear can do double duty, and you can subtract at least one unneeded item from your pack. The mosquito head net doubles as a super lightweight stuff sack—and triples as a coffee filter.

Base weight: The weight of the pack itself with all the items won't change during the hike. The weight of consumables is NOT included; neither is the weight of the clothing worn.

Consumables: Anything that will be used up during the hike. The weight of these items will change over the duration of the trip. They will be eaten, drunk, burned, or rubbed on your face. Food, water, and fuel are weighed

An ultralight camper's
standard calculation:

BASE WEIGHT
(+)
CONSUMABLES
(=)
PACK WEIGHT
(+)
Worn items
(=)
SKIN-OUT WEIGHT

and documented. Sunscreen and other toiletries will get used too, but these are difficult to weigh accurately, and their data is usually ignored.

Pack weight: Base weight plus consumables. The weight of the fully loaded pack at the trailhead on Day 1 of your trip. This is an important number. If you meet a fellow lightweight hiker on the trail, you'll get asked: "What's your pack weight?"

Gear worn: This is the weight of your hiking outfit, meaning anything that'll be worn during the day. This includes shoes, socks, sunglasses, watch, and your hat. This number is hard to pin down because you need to (somewhat arbitrarily) pick your prototypical hiking ensemble. This will obviously change with weather and terrain.

Skin-out weight: The weight of absolutely everything that is going in the field on the trip. The collective sum of your base weight, consumables, and gear-worn—everything! This is a nice techie number to know, but it's rarely used, even by the nerdiest.

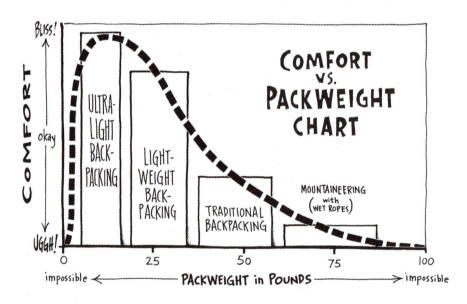

12. THE MODEL TRIP, our example expedition

For our purposes, everything in this book will be based on a template trip concept and will henceforth be referred to as *the model trip*. Unless otherwise noted, I'll be designing the tips in this book around this example. It will be set up as a solo outing.

That way any gear list will reflect EVERY piece of gear required; nothing will be shared. (See tip 23.) Most importantly, this is an ultralight experience, meaning the base weight is below 10 pounds.

- Length: ten days
- Solo
- Three season
- Ambitious

Our example trip is ten days long—a nice length because you can easily carry ten days of food, and the math is easy. There's nothing namby-pamby about this hypothetical trip.

Let's say the plan is to traverse the entire Wind River Range (in central Wyoming). This is a summer trip in a mountain environment, so we need to be prepared for chilly weather, rain, and arduous travel. Daytime temps can range as high as 90 degrees, and nighttime lows could dip into the 20s. This trip won't be limited to travel on established trails; expect some robust off-trail hiking. We'll aim for more than 15 miles per day at elevations up to 12,000 feet in terrain that'll require a little extra oomph. The trip will include cooking food on a stove and carrying ample rations so that hunger is never an issue. The intent is for long days and significant mileage, but there's no need to break any speed records.

Ten days is a significant load of food weight inside your backpack on Day 1. Any longer and you'll probably want to plan for a resupply point somewhere halfway. Through-hikers will resupply every five days or so, but this is a deep wilderness expedition where that simply isn't an option.

Does this trip sound like too much? (See tip 38.) If you are planning for a single overnight, the base weight of this ten-day model trip is exactly the same as for one night. Just move the decimal point over for the consumables, but pretty much everything else should be the same.

13. Get Lighten Up! by Don Ladigin

Don's book is the perfect introduction to the basic (and empowering) skills required for lightweight camping. I feel honored to have done the illustrations for this tidy and unintimidating little book.

The thought of lightweight backpacking can be scary to someone who's never tried it. That's where this book shines; it carefully explains how to shed those pounds off your back in a simple and straightforward way. It can be done without sacrificing the essentials for safety and comfort.

Golly!

LIGHTEN UP!
Don Ladigin

The book is just over one hundred pages, surprisingly small given the info crammed between its covers. The text is direct and to the point, without any "rules" or heavy-handed dogma. Don is a zealot, but he's never preachy.

While you're at it, get *Allen & Mike's Really Cool Backpackin' Book* too! There is a wealth of practical information in this book. Even though the overall focus is on traditional camping skills, the book has excellent info on maps, navigation, bear camping, first aid, environmental ethics, hygiene, river crossing, and plenty more.

14. Don't expect specific gear recommendations

There is a lot of cool gear out there, and more is introduced every day. This book will actively try to *avoid* mentioning any of it! Stuff gets discontinued, details change, and new gear will trump the already good stuff soon enough. If I actually did document specific gear, this book might be meaningless within a few years, or even months!

Instead the tips in these pages will focus on techniques and recommended weights for certain items. All this book can do is plant the seeds of enthusiasm; you'll need to do your own R&D for what works best for you.

15. Most of the pack weight is in a few items

The Big Three is a term used in the lightweight community to describe the items that make up the majority of the base weight. These aren't individual items but actually systems that use a series of items. The Big Three is actually the *Big Four* when you add in cooking gear and consumables:

1. The Packing System

2. The Shelter System

3. The Sleeping System

4. The Cook System (including food and fuel)

See Don Ladigin's *Lighten Up!* for more info on these items.

The take-home lesson here: Deal with the heaviest items first! Don't bother cutting your toothbrush in half until you've made a real-deal effort to get a really light backpack.

16. Never say "It's only a couple of ounces"

Don't say, "It's only a couple of grams," either; don't even think it! Instead, state an item's exact weight. And please don't point to an item and say, "It's SO light." And never EVER say, *"It doesn't weigh anything!"* It absolutely does weigh something.

A couple of ounces is a lot. If you go through your pack and find eight items, each weighing 2 ounces, that you can leave behind, you've saved a pound, and that's a big deal.

Don't quantify things in vague generalities; instead use the actual weight. Declare to the world: *"This CLIF bar weighs 2.4 ounces, and it is an important and useful item!"* Ultralight camping is an ongoing game of refining and subtracting. If you quantify things against the CLIF bar, you can say: "For every 2.4 ounces I leave behind, I can add a CLIF bar."

17. Never EVER guess the weight of something

You know that thing where you put one item in one hand and one item in the other and then bob your hands up and down like the scales of justice in an effort to figure out which is lighter. I know from experience that this does NOT work. The ONLY way to figure out what something weighs is to put it on a scale.

If you have two similar items and need to choose which one to bring, use the scale. Say you have two hats. One is super cute and looks awesome in photos; the other is utterly uninspiring. Put them both on a scale and take the lighter one, even if it's only a tenth of an ounce difference!

If you ALWAYS choose the lightest option, you will ALWAYS be subtracting weight from your back. This makes things super easy—simply let the scale decide.

=

2.4 oz

(68 g)

18. Create a spreadsheet

Ultralight campers used to have a three-ring binder with an item-by-item listing of their gear and its weight. Now they all have spreadsheets. (See tip 10.) Yes, all these numbers get plugged into a computer program.

category	item	notes	weight in oz
GEAR WORN	shoes	lightweight hikers, synthetic	31.6
	hiking socks	low thinny-thin	0.6
	gaiters	dirty-girl spandex	1.1
	hiking pants	quick dry nylon	11.6
	nylon running shorts	simple, no undies	3.5
	short-sleeve shirt	wool	4.3
	long-sleeve hoodie	synthetic	7.5
	sun-hat	floppy wide brim	3.1
	sunglasses	w/ string retainer	1.2
		TOTAL gear worn (oz)	**64.5**
		TOTAL gear worn (lbs)	**4.0**

Set yourself up to figure out the auto-sum for your *base weight, consumables,* and *pack weight.* These are the only three numbers that really matter. Feel free to ignore numbers for *gear worn* and *skin-out* weight.

There is no end to the computing zeal of a modern spreadsheet program; it can be a bottomless pit. Don't get bogged down with metric conversions and graphic pie charts (unless you

10-DAY SOLO TRIP

category	items	ounces	pounds
CONSUMABLES	alcohol fuel	16.4	1.0
	FOOD 1.4 PPPPD x 10 days	224	14.0
10-day trip	**TOTAL for consumables**	**240.4**	15.0
	(a) BASE WEIGHT	128.1	8.0
	(b) CONSUMABLES	243.6	15.2
	(a) + (b) = (c)		
TOTAL:	(c) PACK WEIGHT	**371.7**	23.2

1-NIGHT SOLO TRIP

Most of the numbers are the same as above, only the CONSUMABLES change

CONSUMABLES	alcohol fuel	1.6	0.1
	FOOD 1.4 PPPPD x 1 day	22.4	1.4
1-night trip	**TOTAL for consumables**	**24.0**	1.5
TOTAL:	PACK WEIGHT	**152.1**	9.5

NOTE: Data shown without the weight of a full water bottle (35.2 oz per liter)

category	item	notes	weight in oz
CLOTHING CARRIED	insulating down jacket	montbell inner jacket	7.9
	rain coat	drop stopper	7.1
	rain skirt	home-made	2.0
	long undies	synthetic	4.6
	wind shirt	GoLite	3.3
	warm hat	w/headlamp sewn on	1.7
	extra hiking socks	thinny-thin	0.6
PACKING	backpack	GoLite JAM (trimmed)	17.0
	pack liner	plastic compactor bag	2.2
	stuff sack (A)	for food	0.6
	stuff sack (B)	for cook gear	0.3
COOK GEAR	titanium mug	cooking & eating	1.7
	mug lid (home-made)	foil	0.2
	cozy (home-made)	insulating foam	0.2
	spoon	titanium	0.3
	stove (home-made)	cat food can	0.2
	fuel bottle (1-liter volume)	platypus w/squirt lid	0.9
	wind screen (home-made)	aluminum foil	0.2
	pot grabbers	trangia	0.6
	bic lighter	mini (cute)	0.4
SHELTER	2-person tarp	SpinTwin with string	9.8
	titanium stakes (11 total)	with tyvec envelope holder	3.2
	no poles, I can find sticks	*WEIGHT NOT NOTED*	0.0
SLEEPING	sleeping quilt	golite down	19.0
	sleeping pad	inflatable torso pad	8.0
	bivy sack	vapr brand	5.9
	balaclava	synthetic	1.8
	sleeping socks	shorty wool blend	1.3
	glove liners	thin synthetic	1.1
	pillow	home-made w/ziploc bags	1.8
ESSENTIALS	large water bottle	1-liter soda bottle	1.5
	small water bottle	500 ml water bottle	0.6
	bandana (cotton)	trimmed	0.4
	camera	digital with case	6.1
	mosquito head-net	doubles as stuff sack	0.4
	maps (in ziploc)	estimate varies w/route	2.5
	first aid kit	in ziploc sandwich bag	2.6
	repair kit	in ziploc sandwich bag	1.8
	bear hang kit	45 feet of cord	2.2
	bear spray w/ holster (13.2 oz)	*WEIGHT NOT NOTED*	0.0
DINKY STUFF	water treatment	Aqua-Mira repackaged	1.2
	Hydropel (for feet)	repackaged	0.3
	toothbrush	cut-handle	0.2
	toothpaste dots	in tiny ziploc baggie	0.3
	paper book of matches	in tiny ziploc baggie	0.2
	soap	Dr. Bronner's repackaged	0.7
	hand sanitizer	repackaged	0.7
	single edge razor	w/cardboard holder	0.1
	lip stuff	burt's bees (luxury item)	0.3
	sun block	repackaged	0.8
	small compass	carried with maps	1.1
	ziploc FREEZER bag	holds all dinky stuff	0.2
		TOTAL base weight (oz)	128.1
		TOTAL base weight (lbs)	8.0

think that's fun). Just stick with the basics—sparse is better than complicated.

Do all your gear planning on the computer; meditate over each item listed, and subtract everything that doesn't affect safety or comfort. C'mon, be bold. Then, when you've whittled everything down to the bare minimum, just print out the spreadsheet and use it as a checklist when you fill your backpack. If you were exacting with the numbers going in, your pack weight will match the spreadsheet total exactly.

A list near the end of this book shows a complete breakdown of every gear item you *might* want on a UL trip (see tip 61). Please know, this inventory does NOT match the pared-down spreadsheet.

19. Some items weigh zero!

This is my favorite tip in the book. Lightweight campers will trim excess on their gear to get the weight a little lower. But there is a very uncomplicated way to get the weight of certain items down to their absolutely lowest number, right down to zero! The solution is easy: You simply leave them behind.

Very few items are essential. What can you actually do without? (See tip 8.) Some stuff deemed essential by the traditional camper has no place in the realm of ultralight. A second pair of shoes (or sandals), known lovingly as "camp" shoes, is easily nixed; thus the extra shoes weigh zero. Other items that can be left behind are a sleeping bag compression stuff sack, hydration tubes, sleeping bag liners, a potty trowel, and toilet paper—these all now weigh zero!

20. There's no such thing as "just in case"

Traditional hikers will simply toss something into their backpack and blindly declare, "I'll take this just in case!" I'm not sure what that actually means. There is no "just in case" gear in the UL backpack; if you are taking it, there should be a sound reason. Certain items are essential, like the first-aid kit, repair kit, and (in bear country) bear spray. If I do everything right, these won't get used. But they are not "just in case" items—they are a prerequisite to safety.

If you are strategizing a UL camping trip in the Northern Rockies, you need to be aware that it might snow, even in summer. You'll need to be totally prepared for that extreme situation. You should not pack an "extra" puffy jacket just in case it snows; you should carefully tailor your gear list knowing full well you might camp and travel in snow. I have dealt with a few summer snowstorms with only UL gear, and it has been absolutely fine. I did have to revise my routine a little bit (no napping in the sun), but it wasn't a big deal. Some simple tricks helped, including plastic bags on my feet. (See tip 89.)

Plan your insulating layers for the extremes of anticipated weather (see tip 3). Please know, I deeply value being warm in the mountains, and my choices reflect that very real need. Your gear list should guarantee your comfort, whatever the weather.

That said, it is perfectly appropriate to say, "If it gets colder than I anticipate, doing crunches in my quilt is not a big deal. I'll be fine." So instead of tossing an extra physical item in the backpack, you can rely on a mental item between your ears.

21. Think in systems

No piece of gear should be used independently; everything is part of a system. I don't have cook *gear;* I have a cook *system.* Same with the shelter and packing, and they should all overlap because of multiuse items.

THE COOK SYSTEM

For example: My *sleep system* for the model trip includes the sleeping quilt, sleeping pad, bivy sack, pillow, sleeping socks, backpack (under my legs), my maps (under me), repair kit (under me), first-aid kit (under me), and my rain skirt (under me).

The system also includes most of my clothes: hiking pants, nylon running shorts, short-sleeved synthetic shirt, long-sleeved hoodie, insulating jacket, raincoat, long underwear bottoms, wind shirt, warm hat (with headlamp), thin gloves, and my bandana around my neck.

If I leave behind a warm insulating jacket, can I take a slightly warmer sleeping quilt and save some weight? This system requires me to think a little more—and hike (and stay warm) right up until it's time to climb in for beddie-bye.

22. Learn to sew

UL hikers modify their own gear (see tip 9), and this means embracing your inner seamstress. Prudent use of needle and thread can solve a lot! I have a little shoebox with my gear for my ongoing modification projects. It contains scissors, razor blades, a variety of glues, a lighter (for melting nylon edges after trimming), fabric tape, wire cutters, needle-nose pliers, thin webbing, string, dental floss (the strongest thread), and a sewing kit (with my beloved collection of big fat darning needles).

I figure that I'm as smart as the person who invented the gear, so if I see something I can improve (revise, modify, adjust, revamp, or *eliminate*), I just do it.

23. Teammates help lighten the load

Most UL zealots will log a lot of solitary trail miles. There can be a very real mystical beauty found in time spent alone in the mountains. But being out in the wilderness with a close pal accounts for some of the most satisfying and joyous experiences of my life.

If you are hiking with a teammate, your overall pack weight will go down, even if only a little bit. Certain items become *shared gear*. When you create your spreadsheet, label these items as such.

Scrutinize everything on the list, and note any item that you can share. Examples: cook gear, shelter, first-aid kit, repair kit, fuel, a sharp thing (like a 0.1-ounce razor blade), bear hang gear, camera, sunblock, bug dope, maps, compass, water treatment, and toothpaste. Some of these items will need to be a little larger (like the shelter) and thus heavier. Total up the weights of all the shared gear and divide by 2. This number gets added to each person's gear list.

It's easy to divide a number on a computer screen. But be prepared: It's tricky to actually divide the gear as efficiently. The fact is, you probably can't share the weight of the gear equally, and the correct response is: *Who cares?* Just know that your collective weights will come down.

If you are camping with a friend, it might be with a traditional camper you drag out on his or her first ever lightweight excursion. This can be a very rewarding experience for both of you. I implore you to take this responsibility seriously. You may be changing someone's deeply held belief systems (see tip 43).

Whatever the team—two or more—be prepared for some group decisions and compromises (see tip 47).

24. The human factor

If you EVER say, "But I always take this thing," alarm bells should start ringing! Be aware; we are not robots. On some level we are just a jumbled bunch of tape loops and illogical circuitry. We are deeply embedded with programming and habits. Humans are tool users, and we can cling to things and ideas. The term *human factor* is used by outdoor professionals to define situations where emotions play a role in judgment and decision making.

When I imagine a cartoon of a camper, I'll draw an Army-style canvas pup tent and a campfire. That's the ingrained mental picture we all have of what it means to travel in the wilderness, right? But that image is merely a perception, and that doesn't mean it's true.

Ultralight backpacking is different from our ingrained concept of traditional camping. And from direct experience, it's more rewarding. I dearly love the sense of freedom in the mountains when I can leave at least some of my possessions behind. (See tip 8.)

25. Appreciate the wilderness

Why do we even go into the mountains? There is a reason, and it can be hard to articulate. For me the need is real.

We are all subjected to a lot of unhealthy influences in our day-to-day lives. I feel like these keep me from truly being my real self. Sometimes it feels downright threatening, like I am teetering at the edge of some impersonal identity vacuum. But when I step into the wilderness, I am suddenly free of all those oppressive influences, at least temporarily.

I have looked carefully at my own enjoyment in the mountains. I've done a lot of self-examination out there on the trail, with the goal of truly knowing what feeds my happiness. Here's what feels true to me: There is no connection between my *stuff* and my *contentment*. Sure I need to be warm and well fed, but that doesn't require much.

The less I have, the happier I feel. Some of the camping stuff I do carry is rather expensive and specialized, so I recognize the hypocritical consumer in me. That said, I really do try to use my stuff, and it allows me to enter a realm that's deeply satisfying.

Wilderness is a sort of mystical term, and I feel a very real need to drink it in and appreciate it as fully as possible.

Hiking with a big traditional pack makes me grumpy at the end of the day, and this subtracts from my ability to appreciate the beauty surrounding me. With the light pack, I walk with a lighter mood. I stand upright and look around more (a LOT more!), and this means I see more. I share more stories on the trail. I sing more. I listen more. I smile more. There is less on my back but MORE in my soul. Add a good pal to this, and the experience can be rejuvenating and transformative.

26. Take care of your equipment

This is a skill, and like any other skill, it can be developed and perfected. It's no different than setting up a tarp in windy conditions or reading a map; it is a *skill*.

I've had dubious traditional campers hold certain UL items in their hand and scoff (with venomous contempt), informing me that it's simply too flimsy to stand up to the hellish rigors of camping in the mountains. That's not true. I employ a surprisingly simple technique to maintain my gear and avoid unnecessary wear and tear, and it's easily summed up in three words: *I am careful.*

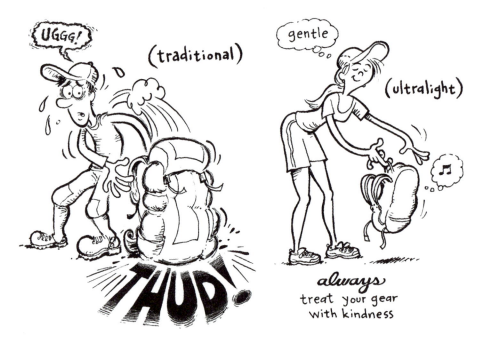

always
treat your gear
with kindness

The traditional camper has an arsenal of Cordura, ballistic nylon, and steel. No need to carefully set their pack down; they can just drop that formidable beast—and then sit on it! Not so with the UL gear.

Everything in the UL camper's quiver is dainty, true enough. But the perception is that the stuff is so flimsy that it's unreliable; some will even say unsafe! I am ever mindful of my gear and its limitations, and I make sure to treat it with loving kindness. Also—I do NOT sit on my pack.

27. Don't lose anything!

If you brought it, it's probably important.

Paring down your camping essentials to the bare minimum means that there ain't much wiggle room if you lose something. If it wasn't truly NEEDED, you would have left it at home.

There is minimal redundancy built into the UL system, so if any one item disappears, it could have big consequences. Every piece of gear should be considered essential. Don't dangle stuff off your pack. Don't hang sunglasses in trees at night. Don't leave your sleeping pad unattended when it's windy! Do a thorough camp sweep every time you pack up to hike. And do a good sweep after you take a break too.

28. Define success

Anyone can suffer with a light pack. The point is to thrive and enjoy the experience. The simple checklist of four points (below) is a good way to rein in your trip planning: staying warm, sleeping comfortably, eating enough to be satisfied and energetic, and not skimping on safety gear like first-aid items and a simple repair kit. All these points can be blended together to meet the needs of any individual trip.

- WARM
- COMFORTABLE
- WELL FED
- SAFE

If you skimp on the tools (or mind-set) that would ensure any of these four simple points, you'll eventually end up unhappy.

Always refer back to this short list if you have any questions. For example: A traditional camper will bring a big vessel just to lug water to the campsite, but the wilderness traveler with a lighter pack can position any cooking near a water source. It's better to leave the big water vessel behind and take an extra warm layer. That layer can ensure *warmth* and *comfort;* the water vessel is nothing more than a convenience. (See tip 2.)

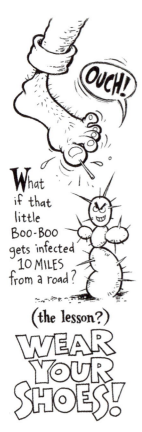

What if that little Boo-Boo gets infected 10 MILES from a road?

(the lesson?)

WEAR YOUR SHOES!

29. Learn from your mistakes

Well, maybe *mistake* is too strong a term. How about learn from your previous experience with a heavy pack? Nearly every lightweight camper started out as a heavyweight camper. The evolution to a lighter pack can be fraught with emotions and frustrations, but little by little, any wise camper will begin to leave stuff behind.

And it's totally okay to make mistakes in the UL realm. I make mistakes all the time, and that's because I'm so eager to try something new that I routinely screw up (see tip 6). But I succeed sometimes too, and I relish the chance to tinker and perfect ideas.

30. Is going ultralight more expensive?

A titanium mug is more expensive than a plastic mug, but that's about it. There is a myth that lightweight camping gear is prohibitively expensive, and the purpose of this tip is to put an end to that false perception!

Lightweight gear is, by its very nature, void of extraneous bells and whistles. There is less materials and fewer pockets and no gizmos; thus the weight, and the cost, plummet. Same goes for tents, sleeping bags, and everything else.

But most significant, the fact that you simply take less stuff (see tip 7) means you are paying $0 for the things you leave behind.

Some UL items are ridiculously cheap compared with their traditional counterpart. Here's an example: You can make a perfectly fine stove from a cat food can, use aluminum foil for a windscreen, and carry the fuel in a soda bottle. All of this is basically stuff gleaned for free from your kitchen or trash. A traditional backpackers stove can cost close to $100, and you need a special metal bottle (an extra $19) to carry the fuel. That's $119 compared to $0.

Most UL campers have fancy-pants titanium cookware, but simple aluminum pots are available in comparable weights at a fraction of the price.

MSR Titan Kettle (titanium) 4-ounce/850 milliliter: $59

AGG Non-Stick (aluminum) 3.8-ounce/710 milliliter: $10

The real gram counters use an old beer can with the lid filed off as their solo cook pot; this is the absolute lightest—and it's free!

31. What does *in camp* really mean?

If you are truly on a roll, using every trick to boost efficiency, there should be only mere minutes between sleeping and hiking. If you are cooking meals on-trail (see tip 70), you can hike

the path is only a metaphor.

till bedtime and quickly climb into your bag and sleep. In the morning, you simply roll out of bed and start hiking again.

With this streamlined strategy, the term *in camp* doesn't really mean anything.

But if you wanna relax at the end of the day (and the next morning) in a beautiful spot, you'll be plunked down in one place for an extra bunch of hours. This is a traditional form of camping, and this lazy zone of dinner/sleep/breakfast is known as being in camp.

If this has been your time-honored mode of camping, I implore you to rethink your standard operating procedures. (See tip 24.) No need to spend time parked in one place. Yes, it might be beautiful in camp, but so is moving through the wilderness with a UL pack. You can drink in that same beauty as you travel.

Traditional campers find their comfort in camp only after the crippling backpack is jettisoned off their back. Ultralight campers find their comfort on the trail.

32. Be present on the trail (a simple exercise)

Stop and look at a beautiful flower. Take a moment and simply bring your attention to it. Do not *think* about it but simply perceive it, to hold it in your awareness.

That flower is connected to the ground as well as the sky; its life and beauty depend on both. That flower is connected to the unimaginably small minerals and nutrients in the soil as well as the vast super spectrum of its place in the mountains. It is connected to the rain that fell yesterday and the bees that will visit tomorrow. It is connected to all the other flowers in the same field. Some are barely budding, while others have already begun wilting; its beauty is fleeting. It's also connected to time. It was

once a seed, and soon enough it will wither and die, melting back into the earth.

That flower is also connected to you. By giving it your complete attention, you are communing with it. Something of its essence then transmits itself to you. You can sense how still the flower is, and in doing so, that same stillness can arise within you. The seer and the seen become one.

When you begin hiking again, look at the bigger picture around you and try to truly appreciate where you are. The simple lesson of a tiny flower can play itself out in the completeness of the wilderness that surrounds you.

33. Ditch the watch, wallet, money, cell phone, iPod, and car keys!

Why do we go into the wilderness? For me, I relish the chance to separate myself from *this* world, and I want to fully lose myself in *that* world. Anything that doesn't serve that separation gets left behind. On a very deep level, I dearly love NOT having these items, at least temporarily. One of the very real benefits of the longer expeditions (see tip 12) is the liberation from news, phones, e-mail, and music. Going on a *media fast* has huge benefits for the soul.

I love not having a watch. It's so gratifying to work off the position of the sun as the day unfolds (some people freak out). If you've never done this, I strongly recommend this very simple challenge.

When I leave my car at the trailhead, I usually just tuck any expensive stuff under my seat and then hide the keys under the bumper. If there are concerns about theft, I'll put any stuff I don't want to leave inside the car in a plastic bag, walk off away from the parking lot, and hide it in the bushes somewhere.

I don't like to hike with an MP3 player, especially in grizzly or black bear country. For obvious reasons, it's good to have all my perceptions attuned to what's going on around me.

I don't carry a cell phone, because most places I hike don't have reception anyway. Am I jeopardizing my own safety? I don't know; I feel like I prioritize my own safety, and I don't want to depend on that small tool. I began hiking in the era before cell phones, and somehow we all did fine.

Now, if you're doing a through hike on the Appalachian Trail, there might be very good reasons for *some* of this stuff, but be mindful of every item. (See tip 8.)

All that said, sometimes I actually carry a watch. It's a dinky $14 digital with the wristband cut off, and I added a string so I can wear it around my neck; it weighs 0.7 ounce.

34. It's okay to stink!

I teach expedition skills in remote wilderness settings for up to thirty days at a stretch. Part of my job description is to pacify novice campers who are preoccupied with being grubby. I try to project empathy, but what I feel is my true strong point is to role model happily sitting in the dirt.

Here's what I've learned: After a while everyone ends up smelly, and that's okay. It doesn't even cross my mind when I'm in the mountains.

We live in a world where hot showers and perfumed shampoo are unfailingly available. There is a perception that we are required to wash our clothes (and ourselves) in any and all situations. Don't get all wiggy if you are temporarily separated from those niceties; you'll be just fine.

That said, I do wash my socks occasionally (for foot health), and I wash my hands at least once a day (for hygienically handling food). And I (sometimes) carry some Gold Bond menthol talc in a tiny plastic vial to sprinkle in my shorts as needed.

35. Make a friend of the night

Greenhorns will turn on their headlamp or other light source as soon as the sun dips below the horizon, and they'll leave it on continually until bedtime. But you can actually do just fine in the darkness; usually there is enough ambient light to deal with the simple chores as you prepare for bedtime.

Some headlamps (like mine) have a cool red-light mode. Your night vision adjusts much better to the red spectrum, and I do most of my nighttime duties using the red mode.

It's also no big deal to log a few extra miles of hiking at night. When positioned on the forehead, the headlamp is perfect for dealing with close-up stuff. But it can create a funny shadow in direct line with your eyes, making for an awkward perspective for things beyond a few feet. It improves your sense of 3-D to move the lamp down a little. Holding it in your hand (like a flashlight) helps a lot, and so does attaching it to the hip belt on your pack at about belly button level. Ultralight superstar Andrew Skurka carries a dedicated strap specifically to position his headlamp midtorso for nighttime hiking.

As a point of courtesy, never look your camping partners in the face when wearing a headlamp in the dark; it'll momentarily blind them. Face-to-face communication is for job interviews. On the trail it's better to act like a nervous introvert and look at your shoes.

I use my headlamp as little as possible. I want to minimize any separation between me and the darkness; I want to be embraced by the beauty of the night. My dinky little headlamp has several settings, and I very rarely use the brightest. Part of this is to conserve batteries, but the bigger reason is that it helps me commune with the darkness in a way that I dearly love.

For our model trip, I would not take extra backup batteries for my headlamp. Just install a fresh set before leaving, and be super cautious about how much it gets used.

36. Sew your headlamp right onto your hat

I only need a headlamp when it's dark, right? And when it's dark, it's usually chilly, right? And when it's chilly, I wear my warm hat, right? At one point I figured that the headlamp and

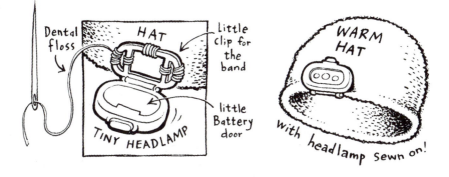

warm hat belonged together. So I just sewed my headlamp right to my hat!

I removed the strap from the lamp (saving weight), and the little bracket that held the strap was easy to sew onto my hat. I used dental floss for strength. The way it's attached, I can still access the little battery door on the back of the lamp.

I sleep with the hat on my head, and the lamp connected to the hat, so there's no need to search around if I need it in the middle of the night. And if it's cold during the day and someone wants to take my picture, I turn my hat around backwards so that I don't look as dorky!

There are lots of extremely lightweight headlamps on the market. Feel free to ignore the expensive options at the camping store; instead look at the hardware store checkout aisle for the real bargains.

37. Mosquitoes and karma

If I'm hiking when the bugs are out, I have some low-stress strategies for coping. I wear a long-sleeved wind shirt with the hood up, long pants, a bandana around my neck, and a hat. If I really feel the need, I'll wear a head net (see tip 58) and sometimes gloves.

HEAD NET

HAT BRIM KEEPS the NET off your face

NYLON Wind Shirt

Bug stuff on the BANDANA around neck

Keep your Sleeves over your hands (or wear gloves)

LONG pants

Maybe I'll use a little bug repellent; I've had good luck with the eco-groovy citronella and peppermint oil combo. I use this stuff on the back of my hands and under my chin. I've used DEET, but rarely.

I have nothing against mosquitoes. Don't ask me why, but they don't really bother me that much. I've camped where they've been insanely thick. I walked 15 miles through a swamp in the Wrangles in Alaska in late June. After that experience, I will never complain about mosquitoes again, ever.

Here's my metaphysical outlook on mosquitoes: I do NOT kill them, no slapping or swatting. For me, these bugs are a mystical test of some sort. Killing them indicates I've failed the test, and the punishment means even more of 'em swarming around my face. If I ignore them, or gently usher them off my skin (and talk to them nicely), they will act much more courteous. All these strategies work beautifully (for me)—unless I'm in a swamp in Alaska in June.

38. Take a little test trip

Don't be timid about getting out there. Don't worry about a ten-day trek deep in the wilderness; that might seem like too

SLEEP

HIKE IN

HIKE OUT

TRAIL

The All-important Mind-set

lofty a goal. Instead just do a one-nighter in some woods near home. No need to dwell on an intimidating expedition; simply find a patch of trees you can get to easily.

I lived for a time in New York City. Just a little bit north of that urban prison, I knew of a beautiful flat spot in among the trees, just big enough for me to lie down. It was easy to get to from the confines of my apartment, and I slept there often, alone under the stars. It can be done.

39. Break the 5-pound base weight: going SUL
[guest text from Ryan Jordan]

SUL means "super-ultralight" and is the moniker reserved for us loonies that backpack with base weights of *less than 5 pounds*. Five pounds doesn't give you much wiggle room for error, so if you're serious about going SUL, you need both extreme discipline in what you bring and, perhaps, some gear that is outside the realm of normal. Here's my strategy:

A. Forget doodads, thingamajigs, accoutrements, gizmos, whatchamacallits, widgets, and other paraphernalia and just stick to the essentials. More stuff = more weight and you only have a 5-pound budget. Here's my list for a cold-weather trip in the mountains of Montana:

- pack (4 oz)
- pack liner (2 oz)
- sleeping quilt (16 oz)
- sleeping pad (3 oz)
- space blanket (ground cloth, 1 oz)
- tarp/stakes/guylines (7 oz)
- rain jacket and pants (9 oz)
- insulating jacket and pants (16 oz)
- cook pot (3 oz)
- spoon (1 oz)
- firestarting kit (1 oz)
- LED light (1 oz)
- water bottle (1 oz)
- chemical water treatment kit (1 oz)
- first aid kit (3 oz)
- toiletries (1 oz)

        Total weight: 4.4 pounds.

B. Be hardcore about the weight of the stuff in your SUL kit. My SUL water treatment kit weighs 1 ounce (it consists of two tiny bottles for an Aquamira treatment kit), my 5-ounce tarp is made from high-tech sailcloth, and my pack is nothing more than a very thin sailcloth bag with shoulder straps.

C.   Start out with easy trips in nice weather. My first SUL trip was out my back door to the aspen tree in my backyard. I hiked 46 feet total (23 feet each way) and was able to use a real bathroom instead of a tree. It gave me the confidence to know I could survive a night with my SUL kit before taking it out into the wilderness. My next trip was in the woods. My third trip was in the mountains. My fourth trip was in the mountains in bad weather. By then, I had my SUL kit dialed and knew that it would perform just fine in inclement conditions.

D.   Most important: Have fun with SUL! It's liberating to know you can be comfortable with gear that is so light!

40.   Cross the line—go out too light

Yes, I encourage you to really push it, to the point where you go too far. If you are game to leave almost everything behind, do it on a one-nighter. Don't get too far from the road, and pick a night without weather worries. I went out in summer, leaving my sleeping bag behind, and just took a bivy sack and no shelter. My base weight was a paltry 4 pounds, 3 ounces.

I was warm enough for most of the night, but there came a point when I had to do sit-ups and crunches to stay warm (see tip 98). It wasn't all that bad, and I managed to sleep pretty well. I realized that sleeping a little bit cold wasn't great, but I did fine. I learned a valuable lesson, and it has made me much less intimidated when I set off into the mountains with a light load. I factor in that experience (and plenty more) when planning, and the overall weight ends up lighter.

41.   Have a GO-box ready

I keep all the essential items for a spur-of-the-moment one-nighter in an old cardboard box. I call this my GO-box.

I keep another smaller cardboard box in my fridge with a collection of camping food all set up in plastic bags with the weight noted on each bag. I simply grab the proper amount to feed my needs and cram it in the pack.

In summer, when the days are long, I can quickly pack up all the essentials for a single overnight and walk out the door. It's a short drive to the nearest trailhead. With a light pack, I can take advantage of this additional daylight and get surprisingly deep into the mountains before sunset.

If you arrive at a trailhead at six o'clock, you can easily walk for a few hours, sleep out under the stars, wake up early, and be home before noon. The work-a-day world should be a little less oppressive and a little more enjoyable.

By simply looking out your window, you can get a pretty good idea what the weather is going to do in the short term. If it all looks good (see tip 94), leave the weight of the shelter behind and sleep out under the stars.

RIGHT ON!

Go Box

I go into nature for my own sanity. It's a metaphysical fix, and even if it's only one night, my spirit is renewed. On a deep and simple level, sleeping on the ground is truly rejuvenating. I love the smell of the pine needles, the sound of the crickets, and the connection I feel lying upon this magnificent Earth. I experience an alteration of my busy mind, and I delight in its result.

The lessons I've learned from this are simple and rewarding. The most important is that sleeping outside in the forest is easy. Grabbing some gear and just going is *always* an option.

42. An overnighter doesn't have to be perfect

These modest outings are a good way to fine-tune your ever-evolving system. As a way to challenge yourself, simply make it a point to always try to do something different (see tip 6). It's fun to experiment, tweaking the contents of my pack on every one of these outings. Cut the sleeping pad even shorter? Leave the stove behind? Purposely head out in rainy weather? These are super valuable challenges, and they'll boost your confidence at problem solving.

Maybe someday it'll all become perfect, but where's the fun in that? These little one-nighters allow you to refine your camping skills, and you'll reap the benefits when it comes time to plan those more ambitious multiday trips.

43. Share your UL skills with friends

Get on the phone and pester your traditional camping pals to join you on an overnight trip. Don't hold back on the benefits of the UL pack; do a sell job and act enthusiastic. You can play the role of teacher and go through their items and tell them what to leave behind. This is easy to do on a one night trip.

But be aware that they will probably never come along. They may really *want* to join you, but the hurdle always ends up being, "My camping gear is all stored away, and it's just too complicated to get it all organized."

That's a pathetic excuse. How much gear is really required? (See tip 41.) What's the big deal? Somehow camping has become a reflection of our gadget-hungry consciousness. In their eyes, it's *complicated* when it's actually very *simple*. We've separated ourselves from Mother Nature, and the simple act of walking out into her nurturing embrace should never be daunting. Jeepers, just cram a few things in your pack and let's go!

44. Practice Leave No Trace (LNT) camping

I care deeply about traveling in the wilderness. I love the feeling of being alone in a pristine environment, and it doesn't take much to deflate that emotional state. My heart sinks when I find even the tiniest particle of trash among the wildflowers. Micro trash = macro bummer. I revel in the wilderness experience, and I want anyone who follows me to experience that same heightened sense of divinity. I have a responsibility out there, and I take that very seriously. (See tip 116.)

For more info visit www.LNT.org.

45. Pick up other people's trash

I try hard to leave the mountains MORE pristine than when I entered. One of the benefits of the very light pack is that I can add things as I hike out of the wilderness. If I find someone else's garbage, I pick it up, put it in my pack, and keep hiking. This simple act makes me feel like I'm doing something good. Sadly, I have to leave some of the bigger items (like a smashed and rusted snowmobile), but I do what I can.

46. Simplify decision making with the UL pack

If you have a crushing load on your back, you will NOT be able to make a decision. Well, you actually CAN make a decision; it might just be a bad one. In a traditional backpacking situation (that means heavy), when it comes time to make any kind of choice concerning the trip, take the big pack off and set it on the ground. If you don't do something that simple, you'll probably regret your choice.

The UL pack can dramatically simplify some decision-making issues.

Here's an example: Off-trail travel can be tricky, and sometimes you get stuck in complicated terrain. The problem solving might require a little scouting. With a big traditional pack, this means taking the pack off and hiking ahead to get a view. It also involves making a plan, coming back to your pack, and

a real life
REVOLTING
lack of
backcountry
etiquette

ewww!

Stinky
smell!

USED
Toilet
Paper

flies

UNBURIED POOP!

an all too
COMMON SIGHT
along the trail!

putting it back on. If you take the big pack with you, trust me, your decision will be lousy. But the lightweight pack isn't a burden during scouting missions because it never comes off. If you find a good option, just keep moving.

Imagine this scenario: Looking at the map, you see two options. One is a little shorter but up and over a big hill. The other is all on-trail, but it involves walking a long ways around that same hill. And looking at the contour lines on the map, the terrain on the back side of the hill looks sort of tricky.

With a heavy traditional pack, this decision could be laborious and fraught with anxiety. The act of hiking uphill only to retreat can be demoralizing as well as exhausting. If you hump a big load all the way up there, you'll be really emotionally invested and thus really bummed out if it doesn't work.

You might waste excessive time trying to figure out a way to "push" the route by looking for a way down a steep cliff. You might succumb to the dreaded *human factor*, and attempt to climb down something dangerous. All of this would eat up time and energy.

No such emotional drama with a UL pack. If the route doesn't work, just retrace your steps back down to the trail, easy as pie. Thus you can save time, energy, and emotional angst with your efficient decision making and your little packs.

Another example from years of teaching traditional backpacking is watching exhausted hikers arriving at the camping area at the end of the day. When someone announces, "This is the camping spot," they drop their enormous packs and camp right next to the behemoths, being too fatigued to look for a nice flat spot. They sleep lousy on lumpy ground and end up poorly rested. With an ultralight pack, that same scenario involves a spritely hiker searching out the most elegant camp: flat with a view. All the while, the load is on their backs—never needing to be jettisoned for a levelheaded decision.

Where do we camp tonight? Is it flatter here? What fork of the trail should we take? Is there a better river crossing upstream? Should we travel off-trail? Should we eat all the chocolate? All these choices are gloriously simplified with the light pack.

Do you make better decisions with a smaller pack? Well, it depends how you define *better*. The process is definitely less stressful, simply because most choices do not require the same energy expenditure.

47. How to make decisions in teams

If you are alone, things are easy—you don't need to take anyone else into account. However, add one more person and it gets a little more complicated. If you cling to all the decision-making duties, things are actually quite efficient (this is commonly known as being a control freak), but don't expect a lighthearted mood to radiate from your teammate. You'll need to share the decision-making process, and that means things will slow down. Add a few more partners, and things might come to a standstill.

SLEEPING
BAG
Worn as a
SHAWL

a.

Having a designated leader can simplify things. If someone plays the role of leader, he or she can make decisions quickly. Usually the person with the most experience will naturally take on this role. If the team is on a high mountain pass as a scary lightning storm rolls in, it's okay for that leader to play dictator. Screaming "LET'S GET OUT OF HERE!" is perfectly appropriate—no need to sit in a circle and share your feelings.

But if you're a big team of ten and need to decide if the last half of a ten-day trip is cranking 20-mile days or base camping by the beautiful lake, you'll want everyone on the same page, which may involve a two-hour campfire powwow. The more involved everybody on a team is during the decision process, the longer it takes, especially on big decisions. But the time can be valuable, because each teammate can clearly share his or her thoughts. The result is a better sense of ownership over the decision by everyone.

Little decisions should be quick, but sometimes they aren't. For any group decision, you'll even have to decide HOW to decide. My advice: Do not underestimate the value of rock-paper-scissors as a decision-making tool.

48. Down vs. synthetic

Being warm and comfortable is required (see tip 28). Puffy insulation in clothes and sleeping bags is an essential part of the UL arsenal. The heavyweight fleece jacket is for traditional camping.

toasty

OVERSIZED
PARKA
to cover
sleeping
bag

b.

carry an
OVERSIZED
PARKA

Down-filled clothing is wonderfully light; it provides an amazing amount of insulation and compresses beautifully. Few things are more luxurious than wearing a down coat on a cold morning, but this critical item requires some care. Most UL hikers have a down-filled sleeping bag and jacket. But down loses its insulation properties if it gets wet. The simple solution: *Don't let your down gear get wet.* That statement is a real-deal responsibility (see tip 26).

Synthetic-filled gear is a little more reliable in wet conditions. But it doesn't have the same ounce-for-ounce insulating oomph as down. And overstuffing (like cramming a synthetic-filled sleeping bag into a traditional compression stuff sack) will eventually compromise the insulating properties. That said, puffy synthetic gear is usually a lot less expensive than down.

49. Upper-body clothing

This is a listing of what I usually take for my torso. If I wear everything (and I do every night), here's what I have on, starting from my skin out: short-sleeved synthetic shirt, long-sleeved synthetic hoodie, wind shirt, puffy jacket, rain parka, and a pair of thin gloves.

The upper body list includes your head too. That means some variation of a warm hat, sunhat, sunglasses, and sometimes a mosquito head net.

All my clothing is quick-dry synthetic fabric, wool, or down. The only cotton in my pack is a trimmed-down bandana, and that gets worn around my neck at night.

50. Lower-body clothing

Everybody has a different methodology for what they wear on their legs. Pretty much everything is optional, except hiking pants (see tip 61). There's a wide variety of systems that work well, but we've all got our unique ways; no need to spout dogma.

Here's what I use for my legs in summer: From skin out, I wear a pair of light nylon running shorts with a mesh liner. I don't bring underwear; the shorts work fine. Next I wear a pair of quick-dry nylon hiking pants, and I might not take these off for the entire trip. The long pants minimize the sunblock needed and make off-trail hiking in the bushes a lot less irksome. I'll add a rain skirt and a pair of long undies for sleeping. That's all.

51. The humble bandana

I take a bandana with me in the mountains; well, most of one anyway. I've trimmed off about half of it with scissors. I'll tie the bandana around my neck as sun protection, neck warmer, and to look extra spiffy on the trail. It needs to be cut so that you can still use the long axis.

The bandana is a true multipurpose item. I use it to filter murky water, and sometimes I even use it to wash myself. No need for a sponge or a pack towel. I do NOT use it to blow my nose—I have perfected a nostril clearing technique that can be done without ANY added pack weight.

This is my lone cotton item.

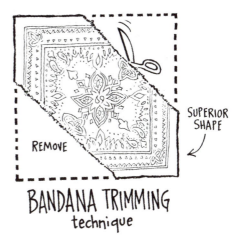

SUPERIOR SHAPE

REMOVE

BANDANA TRIMMING
technique

52. I went camping with no stuff sacks!

None, zip, nada. I did it as a personal challenge (see tip 6), and it was easy. But after going out with zero, I realized I liked to have at least two. I was fine without them, but I chose to add them back to my arsenal of carried gear. This was a want and not a need. (See tip 8.)

Currently I use two actual stuff sacks: one for my food and one for my cook kit.

In bear country I need to hang all these items at night, and using the stuff sacks makes this easy. I like the cook pot and stove (and all the little extras) in one stuff sack because I can just pull it all out of my pack when it's time to make a meal (see tip 70). This speeds things up on the trail when I do a quick breakfast or if I make hot coffee in the afternoon.

I also use a few Ziploc plastic bags as an organizational tool. (See tip 143.)

53. What! No knife?

Not having a knife is incomprehensible to a lot of men. Don't ask me why, but men love knives.

Here's an insight from all my time in the mountains: With just a little bit of planning, I don't have much use for a knife and rarely use one.

The lightest of the lightest is a single-edge razor blade from the hardware store. Even with a homemade storage sheath, this

ONLY 5¢

MADE IN USA

(SHARP!)

Simple ENVELOPE made from CEREAL BOX Cardboard and TAPE

useful tool weighs a remarkable 0.1 ounce! The sheath (created from a piece of cereal-box cardboard) is required because I don't want to reach in my pack knowing there's something really sharp in there. Before you leave home, add a tiny smidge of oil to the blade; the steel can rust.

Sometimes I grumble a little if I have a tricky cutting project like trimming fabric tape, but with a little patience, I can do a beautiful job with my decidedly UL tool.

The one sharp thing I really like (and sometimes take) is a small pair of scissors. These are a valid addition to the first-aid kit, and I use them a lot for other cutting duties.

I found a pair of kiddy scissors (0.5 ounce) in the back-to-school aisle at my local drug store for 69 cents! They fit my grown-up hands poorly, but they'll competently cut a piece of repair tape. Sewing-supply stores are a good place to find high-quality teeny-weenie scissors.

54. Make your own toothpaste dots

Just so you know, those tiny travel tubes weigh in at about an ounce. So this tip is more fun than a true weight saver, and fun counts for a lot.

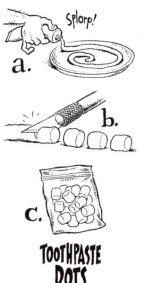

Don't shirk good dental hygiene. Some ultralighters obsess about finding the tiniest tube of toothpaste at their grocery store. But you can forgo the tube altogether and simply dry the paste itself into cute little dots. Chalky white toothpaste works better than anything that looks like clear jelly (avoid stripes and sparkles).

Squirt a long coiled snake of toothpaste out on a plate. Then leave the plate in an out-of-the-way corner for a few days. You'll end up with a hard length of dried toothpaste. Please note: I live at 6,100 feet in Idaho, and it's VERY dry. If you live in Florida, the humidity won't let you off as easy; you'll need to employ a dehydrator.

After it's dry, I use a sharp knife and cut the toothpaste rope into half-inch segments and then let them sit out for another few days. These turn into weird gummy dots and are easily packaged in a tiny Ziploc baggie. Sometimes I sprinkle a tiny bit of baking soda into the baggie to keep the dots from sticking together. Right before bedtime in the mountains, I chew 'em like gum before brushing. Easy!

Another option is bringing baking soda in a tiny Ziploc baggie, but what's the fun in that?

55. Prepare a simple first-aid kit

The list below is pretty much what I would take on the model trip of ten days solo. You have minimal gear, so your ability to improvise with what you might have on hand is drastically different from traditional campers with their extra gear. The following list reflects items that would be impossible to improvise.

- 1 small roll medical tape (multiuse)
- 1 small roll Leukotape (blister care)
- 2 gauze 4×4 bandages (control bleeding)
- 1 exam gloves (avoid contact with blood)
- 3 small packets triple antibiotic ointment
- A few bandages of various sizes
- A few Steri-Strip wound closures (or butterfly bandages)

Medications: All the medications listed below are easily available over-the-counter drugs with a long track record of safe usage. This is a very basic list. It is beyond the scope of this

---

book to address all the potential medical issues you might encounter.

- All stored in a Ziploc baggie. Weight: less than 3 ounces.
- Anti-inflammatories (Advil/ibuprofen or Aleve/naproxen), approximately 12 tablets
- Analgesics (Tylenol/acetaminophen) approximately 12 tablets
- Antidiarrhea (Immodium AD/loperamide), approximately 6 tablets
- Antihistamine (Benadryl/diphenhydramine), approximately 6 tablets

This spartan little kit is not a substitute for proper first-aid training. I strongly advocate taking the Wilderness First Responder course to anyone who travels in remote environments. Please, use your brain to avoid the kind of accidents that would make you need a first-aid kit in the first place.

56. Carry a simple repair kit

Stuff breaks and (mostly) it's easily fixed. Here's a simple list of what I would carry on the model trip.

All stored in a Ziploc baggie. Weight: less than 3 ounces.

- Sticky-backed fabric tape. Most of your gear is fabric, so this is the mainstay of the kit.
- Tyvek tape. Cut the tape into little patches (various sizes) and stick them onto silicone release paper (the peel-away stuff on the back of a sticker, like a mailing label).
- Tiny sewing kit—a big darning needle along with a little needle pushed into a teeny chunk of closed-cell foam. Then wrap a long length of dental floss and a long length of thin sewing thread around the foam.
- String—about 20 feet or so.
- A few safety pins in various sizes.
- Some rubbery glue—a tiny tube of contact cement for shoes.
- Super glue comes in VERY tiny tubes. This can be used for first-aid too; very helpful for dry, cracking fingertips and toes.

57. Trim your maps

Until quite recently, your only option for high-quality maps was the U.S. Geological Survey (USGS), part of the Department of the Interior. But with the advent of the home computer and high-quality color printers, you are no longer limited to USGS maps.

Use the biggest scale you can read effectively. For almost all situations, a 1:100,000 format will serve you fine. If you want to do more aggressive off-trail travel in complicated terrain (like the canyons of the desert Southwest), you'll want more detail, and that's where the trusty 1:24,000 scale really shines.

MAP TRIMMING

Don't be shy about using scissors to trim those maps down to just what you'll truly need. Trim off those extraneous blank borders and any zones you know you'll never walk through. But be careful that you still have sufficient map to navigate out if there is an emergency or a forced change in the route. I speak from experience here. I've cut too much info from my maps, hosing myself because of my overzealousness with the scissors.

Navigation and route finding using a map and compass is a skill. For a good foundation see *Allen & Mike's Really Cool Backpackin' Book.*

58. Multitask with the mosquito head net

The mosquito head net is a true multipurpose item. Worn over the head, as intended, it keeps little flying bugs out of your eyes, ears, mouth, and nose. It makes it almost impossible to read a map, but it may save your sanity.

This simple item can eliminate the need for a full tent in bug season! Wear it to sleep with a brimmed hat to keep the fabric away from your face. Wear a wind shirt with a hood, and pull that quilt up snug. For less than 1 ounce, you can easily save pounds by leaving an actual tent behind. For the really ferocious bug environments, you'll need a few more tricks. (See tip 37.)

The head net also makes an excellent UL stuff sack. It's wonderfully easy to see the items inside, but the net is NOT waterproof. I pack my extra socks, warm hat, and gloves in the head net.

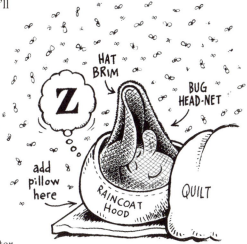

It is also an amazingly efficient water filter when murky puddles are your only water source. Sometimes I carry a little plastic funnel, but usually I can make do with using a cook pot or mug and pouring the water between the vessels. Simply fold the fabric over itself a few times to get the maximum filter effect. Rinse the net out in the same murky water source, and shake it dry.

And it makes a *fabulous* coffee filter, eliminating any complaints about grounds in your teeth.

59. Collect cute little bottles

Repackaging liquids into smaller vessels is an essential part of the UL mind-set. Keep an eye out for any cute little plastic bottles. Once you start looking, you'll realize they're everywhere. There are lots of uses for itty-bitty vessels. No need to carry extra sunblock, soap, hand sanitizer, water treatment, etc. You actually use a lot less of this stuff than you think. Traditional campers will just buy a big tube of sunblock and toss it in their pack. After a weeklong trip, they return home with plenty left over. Monitor how much you truly use, and work backward from there.

An 8-milliliter (0.25-liquid-ounce) bottle is PLENTY of sunblock for a weeklong trip, especially if you wear long pants and a long-sleeved shirt.

Most every home has some drawer cluttered with odds and ends, and sometimes you can score good bottles in there. The bottles for eye drops are awesome, and the smaller the better. Ask your contact lens–wearing friends if they have any extra little dropper bottles.

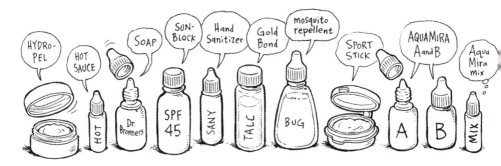

You can purchase little bottles too; they are available in many drugstores and online. If you place an order, get more than you think you'll need. Your camping pals will be envious, and you can give a few away.

60. Select your luxury item

One of the benefits of streamlining every item in your pack is that by saving so much weight, you can add back a few ounces with that one item you really want to bring.

Photographers will perk up when they realize this bonus element to the UL mind-set. They subtract in every other category and add to the column marked "Camera Gear" and then comfortably head deep into the backcountry with their heavy camera.

Me? My luxury item is a tube of Burt's Bees lip moisturizer (0.3 ounce) or, for desert travel, moisturizing eye drops (0.4 ounce).

61. Everything you might ever need

This list contains pretty much every item you *might* need in your arsenal of lightweight camping gear for our model trip. It's meant to be used as a starting point in your planning. Each item has a maximum weight noted in bold text; these are suggested target numbers to help your planning.

Not all these items are required. There is more listed that what you'll truly need, and lots are noted as optional. Many maximum weights are pretty high compared with the very specialized gear available. Obviously, if you choose a lighter item, you'll reap the benefits of a lighter backpack.

Compare this to the sample spreadsheet (see tip 19) and you'll see that the actual items carried on the model trip are much less than the list below.

CLOTHES

- Warm hat. Wool or fleece; watch cap or balaclava. If you have a torso layer with a sewn-in hood, a warm hat is useful but not required. This should be considered part of the sleeping system. Max: **2.5 ounces**

- Sunglasses. Protect your eyes. Max: **2.5 ounces**

- Sunhat. Baseball cap or fully brimmed, for sun and rain protection. Synthetic, quick-drying only. Max: **3 ounces**

- Short-sleeved next-to-skin layer (optional). Synthetic or wool; no cotton. Short sleeves are nice in hot weather and add warmth underneath your other layers. A long-sleeved shirt can be used instead. Max: **5 ounces**

- Long-sleeved next-to-skin layer. Synthetic or wool; no cotton. Zip necks and hoods are nice options. Max: **7 ounces**

- Insulated jacket. Your primary insulation, either down or synthetic; often referred to as your puffy layer. Hoods are nice but not required. An essential part of your sleep system. Max: **14 ounces**

- Wind shirt (optional). Super versatile and breathable while hiking in chilly conditions. These provide a lot of extra warmth for minimal weight. Max: **5 ounces**

- Rain jacket. Waterproof, breathable shell jacket with a hood. Ponchos are an option. The less-durable Frogg Toggs and DriDucks brand jackets are extremely light (and very inexpensive!) but require extra care. Max: **12 ounces**

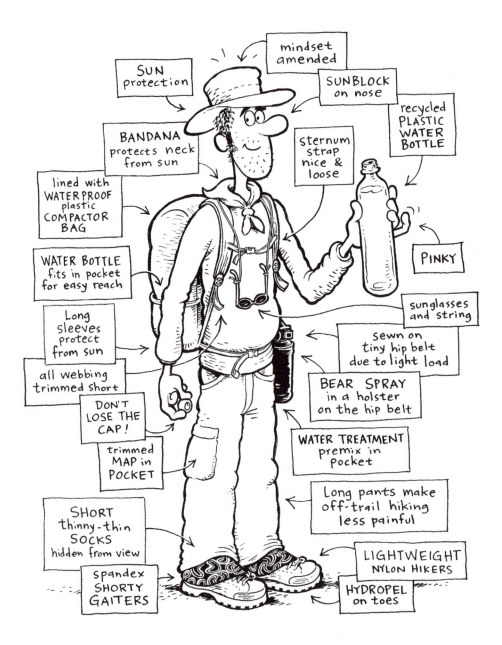

- Extra insulating layer (optional). Maybe one extra shirt, depending on the expected weather. Cold sleepers might need more oomph at night. Max: **7 ounces**

- Gloves (optional). Thin synthetic or wool glove liners. Nice if you get cold hands. You might not use them for an entire trip, but they are delightful on that one chilly morning. A nice addition to the sleep system. Max weight per pair: **1.5 ounces**

- Shorts (optional). Quick-dry synthetic running shorts; act as underwear and a bathing suit. Max: **5 ounces**

- Hiking pants. Long pants made of lightweight, breathable, quick-drying synthetic fabric. Long pants lessen the need for sunblock and make off-trail travel less painful. Convertible zip-off pants are an option, but dorky. Max: **11 ounces**

- Rain pants (optional). Lightweight breathable fabric. Full waterproof protection is NOT essential; quick-drying fabric is okay. Most UL hikers forgo true rain pants. Max: **7 ounces**

- Rain skirt (optional). Functional and cute. Max: **3 ounces**

- Long undies (optional). Either synthetic or wool, these are helpful as part of the sleep system. Max: **7 ounces**

- Puffy pants (optional). Either synthetic or down, scrumptious insulated joy. Helpful as part of the sleep system, especially if you have a really wimpy quilt. Max: **8 ounces**

- Underwear (optional). Some long-distance hikers recommend underwear (compression shorts) for chafe resistance and added warmth. One pair, no redundancy. Another option is wearing synthetic running shorts (see above). Men do NOT need a second pair. Women might find that exercise and change of environment will influence their monthly cycle; extra undies might be helpful. No more than three total needed. Max per pair: **2 ounces**

- Shoes. Trail runners or lightweight hikers. Synthetic nonabsorbent fabric that dries quickly; no leather! Max per pair: **36 ounces**

- Socks. Low-cut running socks made of wool or synthetic (or a blend). Thinny-thin liners OK. Two pairs minimum: one for hiking and another for sleeping. Max per pair: **2.5 ounces**

- Shorty gaiters (optional). No need for waterproof fabric. These help keep dirt out of low-cut shoes. Max per pair: **4 ounces**

SLEEPING

- Sleeping bag or quilt. Quilts are zipperless and hoodless and have an open back for extra weight savings. An ultralight mummy has a hood and zipper. Max: **25 ounces**
- Sleeping pad. A torso-size sleeping pad is all you truly need, either inflatable or closed-cell foam. You'll be using your backpack itself to insulate your legs. Max: **10 ounces**
- Bivy sack (optional). A thin fabric cover for your quilt provides added protection and warmth. Waterproof bottom and highly breathable water-resistant top. Max: **7 ounces**
- Pillow (optional). If you wear all your clothes to bed, what do you have left to put your head on? (See tip 100.) Max: **2 ounces**
- Shelter system (stakes, guylines, and tarp). The tarp with string should weigh around 10 ounces; total weight of stakes should be less than 5 ounces. Max: **15 ounces**

PACKING

- Backpack. Pack weight up to 25 pounds for the ten-day model trip; 50 liters volume, no more than 22 ounces. For a weekend, 36 liters volume, as low as 3 ounces! Max: **22 ounces**
- Pack liner. A waterproof trash compactor bag lines the entire interior of your backpack. Max: **2.2 ounces**
- Stuff sacks (mostly optional). Traditional campers love stuff sacks. Very few are actually needed, and dinky items fit into Ziploc baggies. Max for ALL stuff sacks: **2 ounces**

ESSENTIALS

- Water bottle. Dig a 1-liter soda bottle out of your recycle bin and you're done. How much capacity do you need? (See tip 102.) Max: **1.5 ounce per liter**
- Bandana (optional). A true multiuse tool; your only piece of cotton gear. Max: **1 ounce**
- Trekking poles (optional). Max per pair: **11 ounces**
- Camera (optional). Lots of lightweight options. Max: **7 ounces**
- Mosquito head net (optional). Mesh head covering; doubles as a UL stuff sack and triples as a coffee filter. No wire loops. Max: **1 ounce**
- Maps. The weight of the maps depends on the length and complexity of your route. Carry in a Ziploc baggie. (See tip 57.) Max: **4 ounces**

- Cook system (stove, cook pot, lid, windscreen, fuel vessel). Lots of very light solutions. (See tip 118.) Max: **7 ounces**
- Mug. 500-milliliter volume is plenty. For solo trips, this is your pot (part of cook system), eating vessel, and mug for hot drinks. Titanium is great; aluminum is fine. Max: **3 ounces**
- First-aid kit (see tip 55). Max: **3 ounces**
- Repair kit (see tip 56). Max: **3 ounces**
- Bear hang kits (only for travel in bear country). At least 45 feet of strong cord. (See tip 114.) Max: **4 ounces**
- Bear spray (only for travel in bear country). This requires the extra weight of a holster; putting it in a side pocket is unacceptable. (See tip 115.) Max: **13 ounces**

CONSUMABLES

- Stove fuel. Weight varies (see tip 120).
- Food. Weight varies (see tip 133).

DINKY STUFF!

This is an area where too many campers go completely overboard. When you get right down to it, there actually isn't that much you really need. All the dinky stuff should easily fit in one Ziploc baggie. This list may fluctuate a little between an overnight and a ten-day expedition, but not much.

- Aquamira kit. Repackage in smaller bottles. The little bottle with the premix usually gets carried in a pocket. I'll usually carry this in its own snack-size baggie. (See tip 106.) Max: **1.2 ounces**
- Hydropel (optional). Repackage in a smaller bottle. Use a simple plastic balm jar; no need to carry the big tube. Size it to your needs. Max: **0.7 ounce**
- Toothbrush. The chopped handle is the badge of honor for any UL camper! Max: **0.6 ounce**
- Toothpaste dots. Count 'em out for your needs. (See tip 54.) Max: **0.5 ounce**
- Tiny-size BIC lighter. I've used nothing but a tiny BIC for more than a decade, and it has always worked fine. Keeping it dry is vital. Max: **0.4 ounce**
- Paper book of matches. This is the lightest solution for a redundant way to start a fire. The standard book has twenty matches. Keep 'em dry in a tiny Ziploc baggie. Max: **0.2 ounce**

- Dr. Bronner's soap. Repackage in a smaller bottle. I don't take toilet paper, but I do carry soap. Dr. B's is highly concentrated and comes in an unscented version. Max: **0.7 ounce**
- Hand sanitizer (optional). Repackage in a smaller bottle. This isn't required if you have soap, but I use it sometimes. Max: **0.7 ounce**
- Single-edge razor. The absolute lightest cutting tool; costs less than 5 cents. Max: **0.1 ounce**
- Simple cardboard razor holder. You don't want to put anything sharp in your pack without a sheath. Make it yourself with cereal-box cardboard cut like an envelope and a little tape. Max: **0.1 ounce**
- Lip stuff (optional). This can get nixed if you use a sunblock that works well as a lip protectant. Max: **0.4 ounce**
- Sunblock. Repackage in a smaller bottle. Take as little as you think you can get away with. This usually gets carried in a pocket for easy access. Long sleeves and long pants will minimize sunblock usage and thus the weight! Max: **0.8 ounce**
- Small compass. This usually gets carried in the map bag. Max: **1.2 ounces**
- Headlamp. Lots of high-quality UL options out there; easily sewn onto your hat! Max: **0.8 ounce**
- Titanium spoon. This usually gets carried in the stuff sack with the cook gear. Max: **0.5 ounce**

62. The backpack as a foundation

This is a required piece of gear, and there are a lot of really amazing backpacks designed for the UL zealot. But be aware: You can't find 'em on the rack at a traditional gear store. You'll need to dig around on the Internet to find the real-deal ultra-light masterpiece.

For a weekend trip, you can really push it and carry a backpack under 4 ounces. But for a longer expedition, like our ten-day model trip, you'll probably want something a little bigger to carry the consumables.

- Weekend: volume 36 liters; weight as low as 3 ounces!
- Ten days: volume 50 liters; weight no more than 22 ounces

Get the scissors and go to town on your pack. This is one place where you can really clear away some significant ounces. Don't be shy about committing to the scissors and razor blade as a mode of pack modification and weight savings.

Use a Seam ripper and Undo the rolled fabric on the top

TOP OF PACK

Punch hole every 2 inches

a FEW inches taller

easier to SCRUNCH!

Run a thin string thru like a sailor's sea bag

REVISE THE OPENING of the PACK

SHORTEN all LONG webbing

NIX hydration sleeve

NIX frame sheet pocket

NIX fat string

NIX Compression straps

NIX ice axe system

NIX big hip belt

NIX cord-lock (really!)

REPLACE with thin string

SLEEPING PAD inside as FRAME

TALLER "thinner" opening

tie down points

REPLACE sternum Strap with cute micro buckle

ADD tiny hip belt (just fine with a light load)

TRIM all webbing SHORT

before MODIFICATION

after MODIFICATION

about an INCH long

SNIP!

COMPRESSION STRAP WEBBING

MELT the EDGE

MELT a HOLE

USE a HOT screw-driver or NAIL

Now you have a nice TIE DOWN point for String!

REVISE THE COMPRESSION STRAPS

Extraneous stuff that's easily nixed:

- Hip belt. For really light loads, it serves no purpose, but I like it for the bear spray holster. Cut off anything big, and replace it with ½-inch webbing.
- Any long webbing. Put the pack on with your thickest layers, and trim EVERY bit of superfluous webbing off the shoulder straps and belt.
- Hydration bladder pockets.
- Side compression straps, ice ax loops, extra pockets, and gimmicks.
- Foam pad inserts and their fabric pockets.
- Replace any string with something lighter.
- Cut off any logo!

63. Packing the backpack

SUPPORT FRAME

The ultralight backpack is usually devoid of any kind of foam pad backing to create a support frame. It's your sleeping pad, carefully folded, that creates the internal frame; thus your pad acts as a true multiuse tool. If you use your backpack under your legs at night, the pack itself is part of your sleeping system. In that case, there is a logical reason to leave any foam

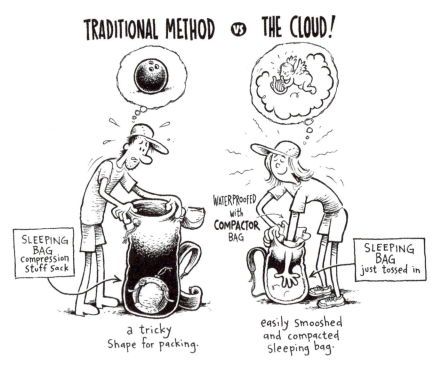

TRADITIONAL METHOD vs THE CLOUD!

SLEEPING BAG compression stuff sack

WATERPROOFED with COMPACTOR BAG

SLEEPING BAG just tossed in

a tricky shape for packing.

easily smooshed and compacted sleeping bag.

pad inside your pack. The few extra ounces will be put to use helping you sleep warmer.

One of the nice things about a (heavier) inflatable sleeping pad is that it takes up very little room in the pack, unlike a (lighter but bulky) closed-cell foam pad, which can max out a tiny pack.

ACCESSIBILITY

Due to the sheer volume of stuff, traditional backpackers need to load their backpack with extreme meticulousness. Everything has its place: heavy stuff, lumpy stuff, and stuff needed during the day. Packing up in the morning requires a grunting game of Tetris. It's all too common for a trad hiker to ignore a developing blister just because the first-aid kit is buried inside the behemoth.

The UL hiker is liberated from these worries. Everything is within reach, and accessing any one item is easy because you can reach your hand in the uncompressed gear.

Some UL packs have a series of outside pockets, typically made of mesh fabric. The side pockets are usually sized to accommodate a 1-liter water bottle, allowing for easy access while the pack is worn. Please use caution when you load these side pockets with gear. Things have a way of falling out, and it's all too easy to loose something because it was crammed in there poorly. (See tip 27.)

COMFORT

The trad hiker has a collection of compression stuff sacks inside the pack and compression straps outside. The result can be a pack that looks (and feels) like tightly packed sausage on the verge of exploding.

Any dedicated UL hiker has no compression straps on his pack because they've been cut off (as they should). The gear in the UL pack should slide in without any grunting and cramming. Imagine the puffy layers as a cloud that gracefully embraces anything lumpy. When the pack is full, it should have a spongy feeling and should elegantly sculpt to your back like a sleeping angel.

One of the characteristics of packing with the beautiful "cloud" method is that the puffy layers have a chance to expand since they are not compressed. In photographs the pack will look pretty much the same on Day 1 or Day 10, because the fluffy goodness will expand to the available interior space.

THE SLEEPING PAD
as the
FRAME SHEET
in the pack

64. Pack up with a buddy

If you really wanna lighten your load, try packing up your gear with a competitive buddy. And when I say competitive, that most likely translates to a guy.

change yer shirt…

ⓐ move pack out front, onto one shoulder

ⓑ slip the other arm out of sleeve

ⓒ hat off

ⓓ quickly move shirt over head

ⓔ hat back on

ⓕ Switch pack to other shoulder

ⓖ Slip shirt down arm

SWITCH

ⓗ open pack and stuff the shirt

easy!

ⓘ return the pack to yer back!

all while walking!

I got started lightweight camping with my pal Phil. We are both pretty nerdy, and we are perfectly shameless about challenging each other to get as light as possible. Decisions about what to bring end up as a game of ruthless one-upmanship. The outcome is a dueling set of pack weights, where each is vying for a number lower than the other. Don't dismiss this very efficient (albeit merciless) form of pack packing. I'll add that Phil always beat me with a lower packweight.

65. Choose bold routes

Always try to cram a lot of cool travel into a short amount of time. Be bold and plan a route that would be extremely difficult with a traditional backpack. Reap the benefits of that dinky pack and those comfortable shoes.

Imagine you are planning a weekend trip; you start walking Friday afternoon and you are all done on Sunday evening. That's two nights and about two full days. How much mileage can you cram into that amount of time? Forty miles (if not more) is certainly realistic. With the UL setup you have the opportunity to experience a significant amount of wilderness travel in just a few days.

The same trip with a big pack and big boots would take double the time and energy. You are capable of drinking in so much more with a base weight under 10 pounds.

66. Trekking poles
[guest text from UL superstar Glen Van Peski]

If you're going to bring these optional items (I rarely use them), these insights will add to your efficiency.

When on a nice level trail, the poles should work in rhythm with your opposite legs. The right pole touches the trail at exactly the same instant as your left foot. The tips should land near your feet and always be positioned so the shaft is angled a few degrees forward, rather than straight down.

Sometimes beginning users "grind" on the poles in an effort to get maximum output from the upper body. However, this messes up the biomechanics of your gait and is counterproductive. Better to grip the poles lightly; and on level ground, use them for balance only.

Going uphill, swing the poles so they are moving in concert with the opposite leg. Bring them up just even with your body, then push off lightly as you take the step with the opposite leg.

Going downhill, change the grip so you are "palming" the pole, with the top of the grip on your palm and the fingers extending over the grip in all directions. This extends the effective length of the pole without your having to stop and physically change the length. Swing the pole in concert with the near leg so that it contacts the ground a fraction of a second before the leg. This helps absorb some of the impact and reduces the amount of load bearing on the leg.

Trekking poles also are super helpful during river crossings.

67. Find your traveling speed

From experience, I've found that my top speed is about 3 miles per hour. I can hike a little faster in short bursts but only with perfect trail conditions, and I don't really try.

I don't run, so I can't keep up with some of the young Olympians out there. I have a nice steady pace that I refer to as *being in gear,* and I can walk like this all day long. No reason to huff or puff. I like to be able to talk (or sing) at any point while hiking, even during long, steep uphills. I use singing to check my pace.

When I'm *in gear,* a normal number for me in the backcountry is 2.5 miles per hour. That's twenty-four minutes per mile in a mountain environment with moderate up and down on inconstant trails. I can go faster, but only for a little while; eventually I'll stumble.

Find your own speed by timing yourself on a defined stretch of trail on flat terrain. A road or sidewalk won't give you accurate data. You'll need to know the distance between two points, like two trail markers. Using a stopwatch, walk that distance, turn around, and walk back to get an accurate time. Don't run, and don't dawdle. Wear your hiking shoes. What is your time? Do some easy math to figure out your miles per hour, and use this as a baseline data point for your trail speed.

There are oodles of things that will impact your overall time per mile, and there is no way to account for all these variables. Any number is just a rough estimation, but this is an OK starting point. Keep track of your own data, and amend these calculations to fit your hiking mileage and times.

Simple 3-2-1 formula:

> 3 miles per hour is fast

> 2 miles per hour is okay

> 1 mile per hour is slow

Anything above 3 miles per hour is *really* fast, and anything below 1 mph is *really* slow.

If you are hiking really fast, more than 3 miles an hour, the stars have aligned. You are likely on a well-maintained trail, level ground or slightly downhill, with the wind at your back; and the birds are probably singing.

If you are hiking really slow, less than 1 mile an hour, you are probably dealing with a multitude of off-trail factors, such as climbing over (and under) lots of fallen trees, bushwhacking through heinous underbrush, slogging through mud bogs, and boulder hopping in steep terrain. It might be appropriate to shed a few tears of despair.

68. Start hikin' early!

When does the sun come up? That seems like a good time to be hiking. Better yet, be on the trail a little *before* dawn.

In the morning, while still in your sleeping bag, start your stopwatch (if you have one). Do this when there is just barely enough predawn light to deal with your gear without using a headlamp.

Get up, put on your shoes, cram everything into your pack, sweep your sleeping site, take down the bear hang, and, when you actually start hiking, hit the stopwatch. How long does this take? If you are even a little bit efficient, this whole thing can be really fast, and that means less than ten minutes.

If it's cold, your pack will be even lighter than usual because you'll be wearing a few extra layers. This is a magical time to be on the trail. It's during these predawn hours when I see the most wildlife, and that's a big part of why I go out into the mountains in the first place.

When I'm hiking in popular places during these early-morning hours, I'll walk past traditional tents all zipped closed. I'm logging miles while those folks are still asleep, and that feels good!

Plan on having your breakfast on the trail (see tip 71) when you find the perfect spot in the sun alongside some running water.

69. Quit hikin' late!

When does the sun go down? That seems like a good time to be sleeping. The length of day varies depending on the season and your latitude. Midsummer anywhere north of Texas can make for some VERY long days where you can get a LOT of travel completed before bedtime.

If I've already eaten dinner on the trail (see tip 70) as twilight descends, I'll keep my eyes peeled for a nice spot to sleep. Usually I'll keep hiking until I can barely see in the fading light, and then I'll find a place to lie myself down on the beautiful earth.

It's nice to do the bear hang with a little bit of light, but you can always toss the rock by the light of your headlamp (I know from extensive experience). I try to position the hang in the direction I'm traveling the next morning. That way I just get up and collect the food and cook gear without needing to double back at all.

If it looks as though it's going to be a nice night, no need to set up the tarp; just lie out under the stars. (See tip 95.)

70. Eat dinner on the trail

Hike until you are hungry, then pick a nice spot (beauty is very important). Make sure you are WELL away from the trail, out of sight from any other backcountry travelers.

Running water is nice but not required if you've collected a liter (per person) earlier along the trail.

Once you find the perfect spot, start your stopwatch. Then sit down, unload all your food and kitchen gear, cook, eat, clean up, and put it all back in the pack. Stop the stopwatch. How much time did the whole thing take? It's nice to have a baseline so that you can factor in this amount of time when planning your day.

I'll eat a little bit early, while there is still plenty of sunlight. I get a real-deal boost of energy after dinner, and I'll take advantage of that energy and log a few more miles before I start thinking about sleeping. During this time I'll fill my water bottle so that I have something to sip on before bedtime. I hike right up until the sun dips below the horizon, and I prioritize finding a heart-wrenchingly beautiful sleeping site.

After eating dinner on the trail, the actual act of camping becomes much easier. There's no need for a water source nearby because there is no need to cook near your tent site.

The stressful issues surrounding bear practice get a lot easier too—you only need to worry about your bear hang. There are no longer any concerns about finding a kitchen site well away from your camp.

71. Eat breakfast on the trail

In the morning, just get up and go. I usually walk for about an hour before I start thinking about where to eat breakfast. I'll hike until I'm nice and warm, and I'll prioritize finding a beautiful spot near water and in the sun; aesthetics are important. How far can you walk before eating? Factor in both mileage and time; this is good info to know intuitively.

Make sure you are WELL away from the trail, out of sight from any other backcountry travelers. Running water is nice, but it's not required if you plan ahead a little.

Once you find the perfect spot, sit down, unload your food and cook gear from your pack, have a hot cup of coffee, cook, eat, clean up, and put it all back in the pack. It's nice to know how long the whole process takes so that you can factor this in when planning your upcoming travel days.

72. Napping is a skill

There comes a point on a long hiking day when I succumb to the overriding urge to close my eyes in the sun. The afternoon siesta can be a beautiful thing. I encourage you to practice this as a beloved mountain skill; I predict you'll achieve mastery, even on the first try.

INGENIOUS NAPPING CHECKLIST

- ❑ Find a spot well away from the trail so that other hikers won't think you're dead.
- ❑ Take your shoes and socks off, and let those feet air out!
- ❑ If it's buggy, find a spot with a slight breeze.
- ❑ If you are in bear country, keep the bear spray handy.
- ❑ Use your backpack as a pillow.
- ❑ Don't get sunburned.

Should you set an alarm? I don't. I find that the entire napping process, from picking the perfect spot to being back on the trail (with sleep in between), usually clocks in at exactly an hour.

This afternoon renewal can be effectively followed with coffee on the trail. (See tip 130.)

73. Hike a 20-mile day

This intimidating number seems to be a threshold of sorts, but it's pretty easy to accomplish. If you get up early and move at a nice, relaxed pace (see tips 68 and 69), even with breaks and naps, you'll efficiently knock off 20 miles with nothing more than good habits.

At 2.5 miles per hour, it should take only eight hours of actual hiking time to complete a 20-mile day. That's a nice moderate speed (twenty-four minutes per mile) that can be sustained without much hassle. So if you start hiking at 7:00 a.m. and figure on eight hours of actual hiking time, you should have 20 miles under your belt by 3:00 p.m., and that's early.

This hiking speed accounts for travel on-trail in moderately challenging terrain, factoring in some elevation gain and some crummy trail conditions.

Let's say breakfast and dinner each take an hour. Add an hour nap in the afternoon, a half-hour coffee break, a total of one hour of breaks, a half-hour swim in the lake, and another half hour of picking huckleberries. That's five hours of chillin' and not hiking, all factored into the day. Add that to the subtotal above, and you'll end your day at 8:00 p.m.; in summer there might be an hour of daylight left. There you have it—20 miles, and in perfectly casual style!

74. Take a break!

The traditional camper will use a watch, hike for an hour, and then stop and rest for ten minutes, except the break usually drags on for twenty minutes or more. When the pack is torture, this is perfectly logical procedure.

I have no idea when or how to take breaks with a UL pack. Here's my strategy: When I feel like I need a break, I just stop and take one. Or if my hiking partner asks for a break, I'll say sure. Taking a break becomes something organic and free form, not a scheduled obligation.

If your priority is traveling and you are stealth camping and doing meals on the trail, then the break on the trail plays a different role. Swimming in a beautiful lake, napping, and enjoying a cup of hot coffee are not the domain of the traditional campsite. (See tips 31, 70, 72, 92, and 130.)

In the middle of the day, when everything is humming, I can happily chug along for well over three hours without ever thinking about a break. Near the end of the day, I'll pause on the trail a little more often, and that's okay.

Break checklist:

❏ Fill up on water.
❏ Treat water.
❏ Eat something.
❏ Look at the map.
❏ Apply sunblock.
❏ Change layers.
❏ Contemplate a nap.

With a UL pack, you can do all those things *without ever stopping!*

75. The art of off-trail travel

If you are on a path, you are traveling in someone else's foot-steps. This can be efficient and delightful but can also minimize the adventure. You are allowed to leave the path and venture into areas that see much less human traffic. When you liberate yourself from the pounded dirt under your shoes, the path becomes something metaphysical.

In some places, off-trail travel is so oppressive and the brush so thick that venturing beyond the path might be close to impossible. The Adirondacks in upstate New York have areas where you can barely crawl, while the northern Rockies have lots of amazing off-trail opportunities above a certain elevation. And in places like Alaska there are no paths at all, except the ones made by caribou herds.

Leaving the established path can be super rewarding, and it can amplify the sense of wilderness enormously. But it also amplifies your responsibility to use the map efficiently, to use your judgment, and to minimize your impact. From my experience, boots are *not* required for off-trail travel; my lightweight shoes perform beautifully. You'll hike slower in most off-trail situations, but the value of the experience is magical.

Off-trail travel requires good navigation skills, a subject not covered in this book. But there is loads of good info in *Allen & Mike's Really Cool Backpackin' Book.*

76. Scrambling is much easier with a dinky pack

With a UL pack on your back and light shoes on your feet, there is an enhanced ability to move swiftly through steep terrain. Decision making, scouting, probing, using hands, climbing, retreating—the ability to do all these important things efficiently is the province of the UL pack.

Be careful, because you can very quickly find yourself out of the realm of the backpacker and into the realm of the mountaineer. If something feels scary, trust that feeling!

I have climbed a lot of peaks in the West. Some have been technical undertakings with ropes, oodles of gear, and a trusted partner. But most have been nothing more than a long, lovely uphill walk. Peak ascents with the UL pack can be joyous. No need to cache gear and return for it later; just plug along with your full load. The light load can make crumbly rocks and some fourth-class terrain a lot less scary.

I've made climbing a remote peak the centerpiece of my UL camping expedition. It can be a predetermined goal right from the start, or I can just be walking through a mountain pass and I'll look up a lovely nearby summit. Right in the moment, I'll decide that it would be fun to stand on top. That kind of spontaneity can be super rewarding.

77.   Traveling on snow as a skill
I teach mountaineering skills in Alaska, the Rockies, the North Cascades, and Canada. I've literally spent years of my life wearing big boots in steep, snow-covered mountains. With these experiences under my belt, I have a high level of comfort on the backcountry summer snow in the northern Rockies.

The ice ax is the mountaineer's insurance in steep snow, and using it requires skill and practice. But the UL traveler will forgo the weight of this tool and use judgment instead. This means turning back if the conditions are unsafe, and that's a great decision.

There is plenty of snow-covered terrain that is perfectly appropriate for light shoes and no ax. Traveling light allows you to avoid dangerous snow slopes by making good decisions and not being emotionally locked into anything on your route. (See tip 46.)

If you find yourself on a steep slope where you truly need the added security of an ax, you need the self-awareness to just turn around. Be aware that having a goal (such as a peak or completing a route) can add an emotional factor to turning around. Don't let yourself feel defeated if you have to retreat.

Something I consistently verbalize when I am in steep terrain is what are the *consequences of a fall?* I ask it out loud to my partner and to myself. What if I fell, right here, or over there? What would be the outcome? Would I slide, accelerate, hit a boulder, or fall off a cliff? If the answer is yes, I simply turn

TRAVEL ON FIRM SUMMER SNOW

around. UL routes need to reflect this very conservative mode of snow travel. It's okay to make some long diversions to avoid any potential hazard.

I truly do verbalize my concerns out loud. This kind of team discourse is all too often avoided because nobody wants to appear weak or inept. Don't make the mistake of keeping safety issues bottled up in your head. If you are thinking it, your teammate is probably thinking it too. "My partner will think I'm a weenie" is NOT a valid reason to keep your mouth shut.

It's always easier to make decisions as you approach steep terrain, because you'll be able to alter your route well before getting into any tight spots. Walking with your head up and looking around is a lot easier with a light pack.

Snow and lightweight nylon hiking shoes are actually a pretty nice combination. You won't be able to kick the way you can with big mountaineering boots, so you'll be forced to use a little more finesse. Expect your feet to get soaked, though (see tip 88), but if you have the benefit of lovely sunny weather, your

Travel Techniques

shoes will dry quickly once you leave the soggy foot-holes of summer snow.

If it's early in the morning and the snow is too hard to make good steps, find another route or find a nice spot in the sun and take a nap until the snow softens up. No need to get hurt taking a big ride on bulletproof snow.

78. No car shuttle? Use your thumb!

In-and-out loops are easy, but traveling from point A to point B can be much more satisfying. Parking a car at the end is a fine incentive to finishing your trip. But getting it there requires someone else helping with the driving. If you are in an out-of-town location and need a shuttle, ask around at local gear shops. There are places in most outdoors-focused towns that deal with bike tours, river float trips, and guided sightseeing. Usually these folks already have a set fee for a shuttle service and good advice on where to park.

If you've finished your hike at point B and you left your car at point A, no worries. God gave you a set of thumbs, and this is a tried-and-true way to get back to your car after a long trip. Hitchhiking doesn't require luck or skill; it is entirely based on karma. Beyond the misdeeds in your previous lives, here are some hitchhiking tips: First pick an easy place for a car to safely pull over; this may mean walking for while to find the safest spot. And always take off your sunglasses.

If you are at a busy trailhead, it's okay to walk up to a complete stranger and ask for a ride. Just make sure they see how tiny your backpack is so they can praise you during the trip.

For our model trip of ten days, there might be some real deal hitchhiking required. If you are in an area that allows for such a long trip, it'll obviously be rural, so the locals shouldn't be put off by dusty clothes and a little bit of stink. And I bet they'll want to listen to your adventures.

79. Wear lightweight hiking shoes

This may be the single most important item on your gear list. There are lots of high-quality shoes out there, so take your time and choose wisely to match the needs of your trips.

The catchphrase for these shoes is either *lightweight hikers* or *trail runners*. Look for all-synthetic materials with lots of breathable mesh that'll dry fast. High-top shoes are totally unnecessary with a UL pack, and I won't even acknowledge traditional leather hiking boots.

The fit should be slightly roomy, about one-half size larger than your normal shoe size to accommodate swelling from altitude and exercise. This extra room will help minimize blisters and sore feet.

Before doing a ten-day trip, do a few long day hikes to make sure your shoes fit comfortably. And be sure to trim your toenails.

80. Lace 'em nice 'n' loose

I see fellow hikers grunt as they crank on their laces with a single-minded fanaticism. I'm the opposite, preferring *very* loose shoes. For the majority of my hiking, I'll keep my shoes ridiculously loose. I like to be able to slide them on and off without touching the laces, like a pair of bedroom slippers. I've done weeklong trips where I tie my shoes nice and loose at the trailhead on Day 1 and then triple-tie the knot so that they won't come undone. Then I do the entire tip without ever retying my laces.

Sometimes if I'm scrambling on steep rocks, I'll snug 'em up a little. Maybe for walking downhill for long stretches too.

What works best for your feet? This is a very easy thing to test. Simply play around with different snugness as you walk. My advice: Go as loose as you can handle and see how it feels. You can always tighten 'em back up.

Combine loose shoes with super-thin socks, and you are set up for trouble-free feet.

81. Do you need gaiters?

These are the mainstay of the traditional hiker. UL hikers can nix these from their arsenal of gear without much of an issue. However, pebbles and *schmutz* (the perfect Yiddish word) can get into your shoes, especially on dusty trails, so gaiters have their place. Remember, your feet are very important.

STRECHY SPANDEX GAITERS
www.dirtygirlgaiters.com

You'll need nothing more than something light and breathable to cover your ankles. There are a multitude of low gaiters on the marketplace. These all seem to have a Velcro front and a string under the arch, no need for zippers and buckles.

Some UL theorists will forgo the string under the arch and sew the fabric right to their shoes, a bit of nerdy zeal that I respect enormously.

Standard Velcro
SHORTY GAITERS

Ultra-marathon runners use simple lightweight gaiters made of spandex, without any cord underneath. These are the lightest option (1.1 ounces per pair) other than no gaiters at all. And spandex means psychedelic patterns.

82. Prevent blisters *before* you need to treat 'em

Blisters are painful, messy, and easily infected, and they can end a trip. They can appear fast, so it's vital to pay attention to your feet. If you are prone to getting blisters, you should know where they might appear and do some preventive work well before they sprout up.

SEW 'em RIGHT ON YER SHOES!

FAT CURVED "SAIL" NEEDLE

The shelves of any pharmacy are loaded with blister-care items. Specialized adhesive bandages, breathable tape, ointments, and funny glue—all these products have their benefits. The accepted standard of moleskin (or the thicker mole-foam) is the domain of big boots and is less effective with skimpy UL running shoes.

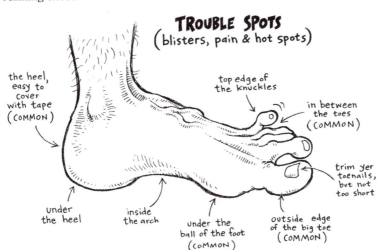

TROUBLE SPOTS
(blisters, pain & hot spots)

the heel, easy to cover with tape (COMMON)

top edge of the knuckles

in between the toes (COMMON)

trim yer toenails, but not too short

under the heel

inside the arch

under the ball of the foot (COMMON)

outside edge of the big toe (COMMON)

There are some neat sports gels, balms, and powders designed specifically to create a smooth friction barrier on your delicate feet. These very effective tools were pioneered by the marathon running community, and they've crossed over into the UL hiking scene. (See tip 83.)

Blisters are much easier to *prevent* than they are to *treat*. Because your feet see so much action, and some spots are almost impossible to tape effectively, treatment can be brutal. I've dealt with a lot of blisters in my career (some were even mine), and I've learned some tricks. I've found that if the blister is small, a standard Band-Aid with a tiny dot of ointment (sometimes I use waxy ChapStick) on the pad is extremely helpful. Tincture of benzoin can add a little stickiness to your skin, keeping any tape in place more effectively. Just rub this liquid on the area you plan to tape.

I can recommend Leukotape, an extra-sticky rayon-backed tape with a zinc oxide adhesive. It's super for blister prevention and maintenance. For more on foot care, see *Allen & Mike's Really Cool Backpackin' Book.*

83. Thwart blisters with Hydropel

Hydropel is a petroleum jelly–based ointment that has proved very effective in preventing blisters. It is also an amazing preventative against "pruney" feet in wet conditions.

The night before traveling, rub a very thin layer on any suspect areas where you might encounter blisters and a very thin layer again in the morning. If you want to play scientist, just do one foot for a few days and monitor for any benefits. This is fun, and very informative.

During the hiking day, if you sense any kind of hot spot or rubbing, stop and deal with it. Applying a thin layer of Hydropel to the area will usually solve any problem. I feel strongly that using this ointment can dramatically reduce blisters and thus minimize the amount of tape and doctoring required to deal with feet in the field.

People with ongoing foot care needs might add a tiny dab at night and a little more in the morning to prevent blisters.

If a blister does appear after applying Hydropel, the area might feel a bit too slippery for the tape to stick. Simply wash the foot with a little soap and water.

For pruney feet, add a very thin layer of Hydropel under the entire foot at night before bedtime and again in the morning. This has proved to be enormously beneficial for eliminating the creepy cadaver-foot effect when hiking in wet terrain. (See tip 87.)

Feet

84. Upgrade your foot beds

The standard foot bed that comes in your shoe is probably gunna be fine. But I love my feet, and there are lots of options that just plain feel better. Every camping store has an aisle of fancy-schmancy after-market foot beds. These come in beautifully art-directed packaging and can be ridiculously expensive. Some even require a certified technician to heat and melt them to exactly fit the individual nuances of your feet.

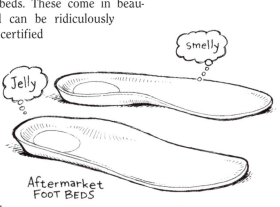

I've had better luck at the grocery store (or pharmacy) for my foot needs. There are cheaper foot beds available in the same aisle with foot powder and little corn pads. I use the rubbery "jelly" pads. I find that the weird squishy material under my feet is essential to eliminating that sore-foot feeling at the end of a long day. They cost about 16 bucks a set, and they're easily trimmed to fit your shoes.

85. How many socks?

This question comes up all the time, and there is no right answer. A lot of ultralight enthusiasts will dogmatically proclaim: "One pair for hiking, one pair for sleeping, and that's all!" This is a very nice mantra, but it's not a rule.

Your feet are VERY important, so it might be wise to take exactly what you need for happy feet. Realistically, socks don't really weigh that much. You could easily cut something off your pack to make up for the weight of an extra pair if you felt guilty about wanting them.

On the rack at your mainstream outdoor retailer, you'll find a ridiculous variety of socks that are actually labeled as HIKERS.

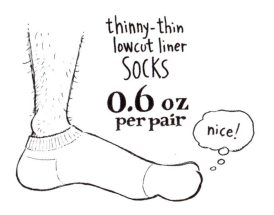

These are for the traditional backpacker; they are thick and tall, designed for wearing inside boots. Instead do your shopping at a specialized running store. The ultralight hiker needs nothing more than the extremely cute shorty-short running socks worn by marathon runners.

I've found that my feet do just fine when I hike with the thinnest little shorty running socks. These weigh in at a paltry 0.6 ounce; I haven't found anything lighter! I refer to these as my thinny-thin socks. They dry a *lot* faster than thicker hiking socks, so I have no problem simply walking through shallow streams.

Do some test trips with a series of socks and get some accurate data about the very particular needs of your feet. If you need to, walk into the mountains with ten pairs of socks and try every pair. Walk through streams and then hike with soggy shoes. Make notes, ponder what feels good, and use what you learn to make a good (and extremely personal) decision.

For a short trip (three days or so), you will do just fine with two pairs of socks: one pair for hiking and the other for sleeping. For a longer trip, I might add an extra pair. Adding an extra set of thinny-thin socks is a guilt-free bit of decadence, because the weight is minimal.

86. Sleeping socks

I bring one pair of socks specifically for sleeping. These are a wool blend, a bit thicker and slightly roomy. I want to spend my time in the sleeping bag with warm, dry feet, and I don't want

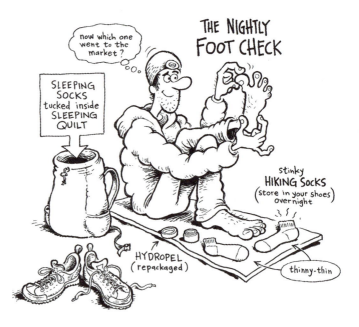

any constriction. These socks are multiuse because I can hike in them too, especially on the last day of a trip.

Here's a typical bit of my sock logic: When I lie down on my pad and prepare to sleep, I take off my thinny-thin socks and put them in my pants pocket, even if they are a little damp. If they are sopping wet, I stick them in my shoes instead. I take a moment to inspect my feet, checking for blisters, hot spots, and dirt. I'll do a little cleaning, usually with the socks I took off or maybe with a bandana. If there is a need, I'll smear a little bit of Hydropel onto any spots that might be showing signs of friction. I prefer to do this at bedtime. Then I put on my sleeping socks and enjoy the night.

When I wake up in the morning, I change back into my thinny-thin socks and keep my sleeping socks dry. A good place to store my sleeping socks is right in the sleeping bag, the one place I know I'll be using them and a place where they won't get lost.

87. It's okay to have wet feet!
Ducks have wet feet all the time and they do fine—and they are downright adorable!

I do NOT carry extra stream-crossing shoes. I do NOT squeeze my socks out if my feet get wet. I do NOT walk barefoot across streams. I do NOT scout for a dry steam crossing. (Well, sometimes I do. But if I don't find it in the first few seconds, I just get my feet wet.)

If you are lightweight camping, you have light nylon shoes. These will dry fast, especially if you wear thinny-thin socks (see tip 85).

If you get to a stream crossing that involves wet feet, there is probably gunna be another soon after, so you might as well expect to get your feet wet. The beautiful thing is that once you get your feet wet (like ducks), then the next stream you find is not a dilemma at all. All moral issues about sacred dry feet are solved once they get that first soaking. If you plan on having wet feet all day, a thin coating of Hydropel in the morning is hugely beneficial for minimizing the dreaded pruney feet. (See tip 83.)

Rock-hopping across a river with a big traditional backpack can be hazardous. But with agile little shoes and a UL load, it's much easier. There is a safety issue when the rocks get big, and the consequences of a fall get more dangerous. When in doubt, get your feet wet.

Please note, when I talk about stream crossings, I am not describing fast-moving rivers where a fall could be fatal. For more detailed safety info on rivers, read *Allen and Mike's Really Cool Backpackin' Book.*

88.   Wear neoprene socks for soggy hiking

Endless travel in a wet environment can take a toll on your feet. Even with thinny-thin quick-drying socks (see tip 85), your feet will stay soggy in rainy weather. This is all well and good on the trail when you are moving and warm, but wet feet will make you feel cold when you stop. When you reach a campsite, you can change out of your wet socks and slip on a pair of neoprene socks. This will help make your feet feel dramatically warmer.

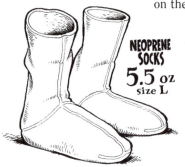

NEOPRENE SOCKS

5.5 oz size L

(2 mm thick with a fuzzy interior)

Neoprene socks are used by fishermen and whitewater boaters. Made of that spongy wet suit material, they provide a lot of insulation and a waterproof barrier. Put them on right over your bare foot, no need for a liner sock. Your feet might still be wet, but they'll be *warm* and wet. A pair of large neoprene socks should weigh in at about 5.5 ounces. I make good use of neoprene socks in the soggy tundra of Alaska. This is a place with lots of rain, and the ground under your feet can be boggy and spongy, even on a clear day. You can easily hike in your neoprene socks, and this is a great option for travel in snow with lightweight hikers.

Gore-Tex and SealSkinz socks are both excellent choices to solve the same issues as neoprene, but they are more expensive and break down over time.

89.   Plastic bags on your feet in wet conditions

Another option for warm feet is a pair of humble plastic bags, and the standard bread bags work best. If you want warm feet in camp, take off your soaking-wet shoes and your soggy socks, put on a pair of dry socks, put plastic bags OVER your dry socks, and then put them back in your shoes. This extremely simple setup provides an impressive amount of extra warmth. Plastic bags basically do the same job as neoprene socks, but they are much lighter and essentially free.

No need to turn tail and run if you get a summer snowstorm in the northern Rockies. You'll be hiking in cold, wet shoes, but you can still keep your feet warm. I've hiked long stretches on cold snowy days with plastic bags, and they truly kept my feet a lot warmer. The bread bags will usually get some holes in 'em within the first few miles. Alas, they'll end up as trash if they get damaged. If you expect some occasional cold, soggy conditions, add a set of bread bags to your gear list.

The coldest my feet have ever been while lightweight camping was on a calm, clear August morning in Wyoming's Wind River Range. We camped in a perfectly beautiful meadow with tall yellow grass. In the cool temps of early morning, that grass was dripping with dew, and walking off-trail felt like someone was squirting my feet with liquid oxygen. I put plastic bags on my feet, and they helped a lot.

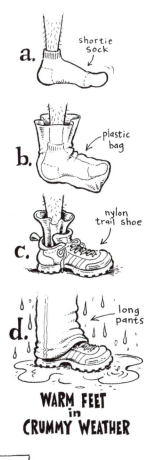

a. shortie sock

b. plastic bag

c. nylon trail shoe

d. long pants

WARM FEET
in
CRUMMY WEATHER

90. The joys of the tarp & bivy combo

When you eliminate the tent and embrace the tarp, you end up much closer to the natural world. The sights, smells, and sounds of the night are no longer shielded but are embracing you. Pitching a tidy tarp requires just a little bit of practice, and the backyard is the perfect training ground. There are a lot of well-designed tarps, and it would be impossible to address all

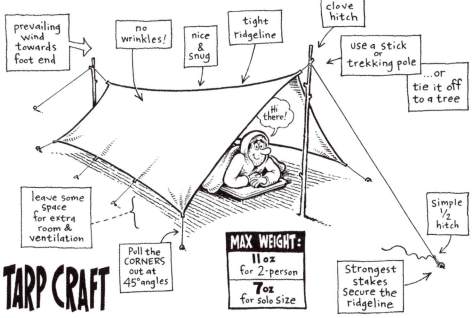

prevailing wind towards foot end

no wrinkles!

nice & snug

tight ridgeline

clove hitch

use a stick or trekking pole

...or tie it off to a tree

Hi there!

leave some space for extra room & ventilation

Pull the CORNERS out at 45° angles

Simple ½ hitch

Strongest stakes secure the ridgeline

MAX WEIGHT:
11 oz for 2-person
7 oz for solo size

TARP CRAFT

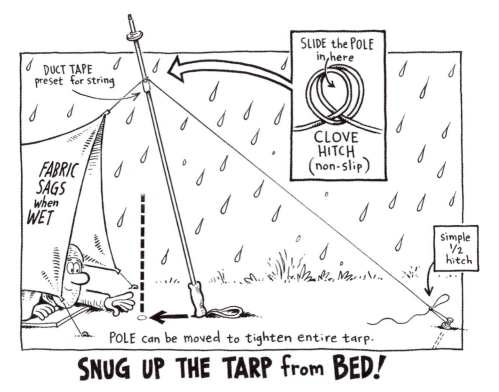

DUCT TAPE preset for string

SLIDE the POLE in here

CLOVE HITCH (non-slip)

FABRIC SAGS when WET

simple 1/2 hitch

POLE can be moved to tighten entire tarp.

SNUG UP THE TARP from BED!

of them. My advice is to earnestly tinker and problem-solve well before you need to set yours up in a storm.

If you use trekking poles, they might be helpful (or required) to set up the tarp. While tinkering in the yard, mark the position where any string might get attached and, if need be, create a little ring out of duct tape.

When setting up the tarp, make the pole at the *nose* end a little longer than you need; set it up at an angle, with the point on the ground being away from you. Then if the shelter "relaxes" or sags slightly during the night, you can just reach out of your bivy and pull the bottom of the pole toward you. That will increase the height and tighten up the shelter pitch.

If you don't use trekking poles, it's okay to use a nice straight stick. But figure out the height during the tinkering process. Just size the stick up to your body. My tarp needs to be

TO TARP

TIED to the RIDGELINE

SLIPPERY HALF HITCH

loop of string tied to the stake

NAIL STAKE buried to the hilt!

15°

angled back approx 10° to 15°

tied off at belly-button height at the nose and a few inches above my knees at the tail. Easy.

Does tarp camping requires a bivy sack too? Not really, but the two in combination can be very nice. I've slept under some *very* small tarps during some real-deal rain storms, and I was happy to have the bivy. (See tip 96.)

The tarp in combo with a bivy sack solves a lot for the sleeper in the mountains. Most bivy sack designs have a waterproof bottom and a highly breathable water-resistant top. This combo provides a lot of protection against the minimal raindrops that might splash in under the edge of the tarp.

Another option is to ditch the bivy (saving a few ounces) and add that weight back in with a larger tarp.

91. Staking out your tarp

These are vital for a perfect shelter setup. Titanium stakes (0.2 ounce each) are very light and strong, but they are pricey.

The standard aluminum version is double the weight but way less expensive. This is an easy place to save money and not be stressed about the minimal added ounces. The cost-to-weight ration might not seem worth it.

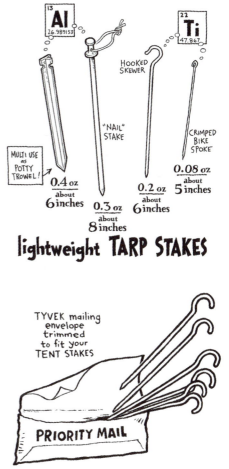

lightweight TARP STAKES

The ridgeline of a standard tarp will require something extra sturdy to keep the system taught and beautiful. Some folks (like me) carry two longer stakes just for the stout requirements of the nose and tail tie-out points. The aluminum "nail" stake is the norm.

On a calm night, the tie-outs along the sides of a tarp aren't all that important; they don't really bear much of the load that supports the shelter. But they help a lot when it's windy, or if you want to position the shelter low in a storm. These side tie-outs require only a piddly little stake. I made a few from titanium bicycle spokes.

Be careful anytime you put something sharp in your backpack. All your UL gear can be easily damaged, and you don't want to poke a hole in your sleeping pad. The lightest tool for carrying your pointy tarp stakes is a Tyvek mailing envelope. No need to buy one; just pull one out of the trash at the post office.

- Titanium stakes (0.2 ounce each)
- Aluminum stakes (0.4 ounce each)

Ahhh... I love my wilderness experience!

out of view!

NEUTRAL COLOR tarp

100 YARDS from TRAIL

no need to cook at the site

when leaving camp restore the area so it looks like no one EVER camped there

STEALTH CAMP

92. Stealth camping as a skill

You can avoid established (and often heavily impacted) camp-sites along the trail and instead spend the night off-trail, well away from other hikers. There is a heightened freedom with the light pack, and that means you can choose where you sleep without having to deal with the burdens of the traditional back-pack (see tip 31). A true UL technician will have already eaten dinner on the trail, so there will be no need to cook at your sleeping site. If you plan ahead even a little bit, there will be no need for running water either.

Stealth means you are well hidden from anyone who might see you from a trail. To me this is very important, because it allows other campers to enjoy the sensation of solitude in the wilderness.

With light shoes and a light load, it should be easy enough to sneak well off-trail and discover the perfect place to sleep. And without a kitchen or tent, the area can be very small. (See tip 93.)

If it's a calm, clear night, you won't need the tarp (except as a pillow). In the morning, make sure to leave your one-night campsite as pristine as you found it so that you won't impact another hiker's experience.

(For more info on stealth camping, read Don Ladigin's *Lighten Up!*)

93. Find the ideal sleeping spot

Traditional campers don't need to worry about finding a nice flat spot to sleep. They just hike to a heavily impacted desig-nated site that's already pounded flat. Then (after they set up their tent) they just unroll their porky full-length inflatable pad, fill a stuff sack with all the clothes they take off, and use this as their pillow. Then they climb into their beefy sleeping bag. If there is something lumpy under them, no worries; they

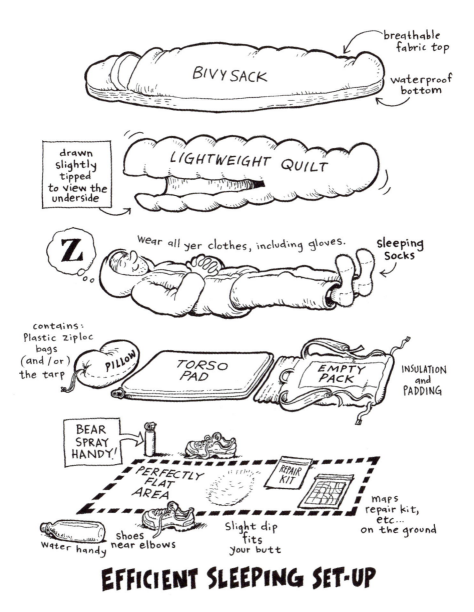

EFFICIENT SLEEPING SET-UP

can pad the spot with extra gear in their tent, like their bulky pile vest.

The UL camper needs to *think* before sleeping.

I am 6 feet tall and about 18 inches wide. I need a flat spot that matches those specifications and NOTHING more. That's pretty easy to find, even in the lumpiest parts of our planet. This means you are essentially able to sleep pretty much ANY-WHERE. You are no longer burdened by the traditional needs of a porky tent. Please be aware that there are regulations in

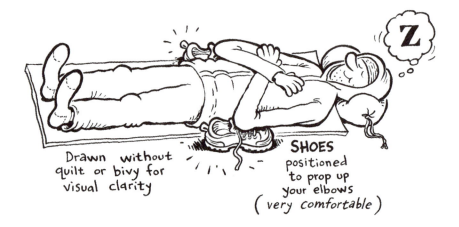

Drawn without quilt or bivy for visual clarity

SHOES positioned to prop up your elbows (very comfortable)

little doughnut as a hip pad

about 5"

made from a scrap of sleeping pad FOAM

use an EXACTO-KNIFE to get the beveled edge

approx 0.2 oz

place in most popular camping areas; know these rules before you set out. Also, it is considered a courtesy to camp well away from trails, away from lakes and streams, and out of other camper's majestic views. (See tip 92.)

You can employ an uncomplicated methodology to test flatness of any potential sleeping zone. Simply lie down in the desired spot; you'll know right away if it's lumpy or tilted. This is a foolproof technique, and I advocate it emphatically. If you are with partner, both of you should lie down side by side.

If you want a little extra comfort, find a spot with a very slight dip at your hips so that your tired butt can be cradled by the loving embrace of Mother Earth.

If you are using just a really thin pad, add a simple little doughnut made from closed-cell sleeping pad foam. This can be positioned under your hip bone if you are a side sleeper.

Okay, you've picked your spot and tested it for flatness by lying down. While you are still on the ground, fastidiously mark out the four corners of your rectangle with some sticks or rocks. This way you can still visualize the area when you stand up and can erect your tarp to precisely cover that zone.

94. Employ the LATS technique of weather prediction

It's nice to be familiar with the weather patterns in the area of your camping trip, but there's no need for a satellite uplink to the National Weather Service. I've found that foul weather rarely surprises anyone. You will (almost) always have a lot of clues for a fairly accurate prediction, even if it's only an hour in advance.

I use the acronym LATS to assess the potential for a change in weather. It stands for "Look At The Sky." If it's gunna rain, you don't need to be a meteorologist; you can usually tell. This

To TARP, or NOT to TARP?

very simple mnemonic tool helps me decide whether I'll set up a tarp or sleep out under the stars. The success rate is pretty good, but on rare occasions I get wet.

95. It's okay to sleep under the stars

I use my tarp every time I sleep in the mountains, mostly as a pillow. I will use any excuse to sleep out under God's magnificent nighttime sky; I love it more than words can say.

If it starts to rain on me in the middle of the night, SO WHAT! I get up and pitch the tarp by headlamp. I've done this enough times that it's not an issue. I can do it in my sleep—well, almost.

I'll usually hike right up until sundown and use the last few moments of twilight to prep for sleeping. During the final few hours of hiking, I'll contemplate the potential for foul weather during the night by using the LATS technique. (See tip 94.) Be assured, if it's a nice evening with a clear sky, I'm sleeping out!

If I'm confident about a clear night, I just lie down and sleep. If there "might" be a chance for rain, I will scout out a nearby place to pitch the tarp, looking for trees to tie off the guylines. I will even lie down to make sure I can visualize the flattest spot in the dark. This takes only a moment and has saved me on numerous occasions. Sometimes (if I suspect

EVERYTHING can fit inside the bivy sack.
(a tidy option)

---

rain) I even set up my tarp and have it ready and then sleep nearby.

If the rain starts in the wee hours just before dawn, I might pack up and hike in the dark for a while. This can be quite a beautiful experience; the time just before sunrise is magical.

96. Sleeping bags, quilts, & bivy sacks— what's the difference?

We all know what a sleeping bag is, and some are even light enough to be considered part of a UL sleep system. The lightest bags will forgo the zipper, requiring the sleeper to squirm a little just to get inside; this is referred to as *condom fit.* A sleeping bag can be very nice if you expect low temperatures; the hood and full coverage are a real advantage. If you do use a sleeping bag, you can subtract a little from your insulating clothing layers because you'll always have a guaranteed place to hunker down if it gets really cold.

The quilt is the mainstay of the dedicated UL camper. Unlike a sleeping bag, the quilt doesn't have a bottom under the torso where the insulation would be squashed flat by the sleeper. Quilts are a little tricky if you roll around a lot at night; it requires an extra bit of attention to keep the insulation positioned on top.

The quilt in combo with a bivy sack solves a lot for the sleeper in the mountains. (See tip 90.) Most bivy sack designs have a waterproof bottom and a highly breathable water-resistant top. This combo provides a little extra warmth, especially if you are using a quilt. It also serves as a waterproof ground cloth, keeping dirt and mud off the sleeping bag. And it makes for a giant stuff sack for the quilt and any insulating warm layers inside your backpack.

Getting in and out of the bivy sack is a little bit like being a contortionist worm. It involves some excessive wiggling. My advice for getting inside is to keep your arms out until your feet are pressed snug against the inside bottom of both the bivy and the quilt. This requires doing a quick, seated bounce on your pad and, in that microsecond, sliding the bivy fabric under your butt. Repeat as necessary.

Some people put their sleeping pad inside the bivy. I've found this works best only if you have a full-length inflatable pad; shorter pads can slip around inside and migrate during the night. I sleep inside the quilt, inside the bivy, and on top of the pad.

For our model trip, a temperature rating of 40 degrees Fahrenheit on the quilt should be fine. But how do you quantify that number? No good answers here. There are lots of factors, including your clothing, shelter, pad, if you have a bivy sack, age, gender, experience, metabolism, relative humidity, weather, and what you had for dinner. The manufacturer's rating is only a ballpark number, but it at least gives you a number to compare.

97. The essential sleeping pad

Your sleeping pad is a true multiuse item because it'll be part of your sleep system *and* the support frame of your backpack. (See tip 63.)

I get a wonderful night's sleep with a torso-length inflatable pad (8.7 ounces and 32 inches long). This little beauty is designed to fit only from my shoulders to my butt. I need to pad my head, as well as my legs. I use a pillow under my head (see tip 100) and my empty pack under my legs. The problem is that I've removed any frame padding from my pack (as I should), so the empty pack is pretty thin.

Here's a solution: I've taken my inflatable torso pad and carefully glued an extra length of thin (5-millimeter-thick)

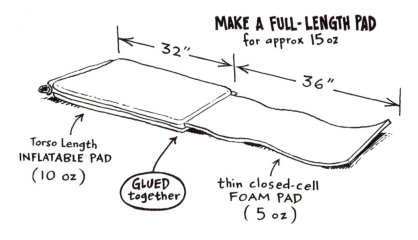

MAKE A FULL-LENGTH PAD
for approx 15 oz

32"

36"

Torso Length
INFLATABLE PAD
(10 oz)

GLUED together

thin closed-cell
FOAM PAD
(5 oz)

---

closed-cell foam to match my full height less my head, which is on the pillow. Now I have an almost full-length pad for only 13.9 ounces. That's considered pretty heavy by UL standards, but the extra insulation allows me to take a lighter quilt.

The sleeping pad is a place where you can really go light (down to 3.8 ounces is a good target number), as long as your weary bones can handle the ounce-shaving pad. Comfort with the thinnest foam pads depends a lot on finding the perfect spot on the ground.

I can forgo the comfort and extra weight of the inflatable pad and simply use a closed-cell torso-length foam pad (4.6 ounces). But I yearn for that extra luxury when I sleep without the inflatable version. That said, the lighter option is fine for summer.

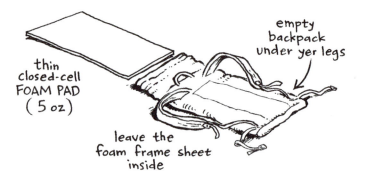

thin closed-cell FOAM PAD (5 oz)

empty backpack under yer legs

leave the foam frame sheet inside

My repair kit has fabric tape and glue in case I puncture the pad in the field. I've had to fix 'em, and it's easy. Still, I am *very* careful to inspect my sleeping spot for sharp thorns and pointy rocks before I set the pad down. (See tip 26.)

98. Sleep warm with minimal gear

The traditional camper doesn't need to think about sleeping warm, he just uses the ample magnitude of gear to insulate himself from the environment. Yes, the traditional can be seductively comfortable in camp—not so on the trail. (See tip 31.)

With minimal gear, you'll need to employ a multitude of tiny tricks to ensure a cozy night of sleep. If you anticipate a cold night, you'll know it before the sun goes down. Use your best judgment to pick a warm sleeping spot.

Open meadows surrounded by gentle hills can be heartbreakingly beautiful, but the cool air will collect in these low areas, so camp just a little bit uphill. Getting even slightly off the meadow floor will ensure a warmer air temperature on a calm night. Dew will collect in low areas, especially if there is a water

source nearby. Get up above the meadow floor to avoid getting unnecessarily damp during the night.

Dense trees are warmer than an open meadow. If you predict a cold night, tuck yourself into a tightly packed zone of foliage. All you need is a flat area big enough to lie down, nothing more. Remember, the coldest nights are the clearest (less chance of rain); it'll be warmer if it's cloudy (an indicator to set up the tarp).

It's okay if you have to do some sit-ups at night to fend off the cold. A few minutes of abdominal crunches in the quilt will dramatically boost your internal body temperature. If you go out for ten days and need to do some exercises on just one chilly night, you've done great. If you need to do 'em every night, you've skimped on warm layers.

More tips:

- What if it rains? Don't sleep in a low area that could turn into a pond.
- Which way is the wind blowing? Position yourself with your feet pointed into the oncoming wind.
- Climb in bed warm. This might mean doing some jumping jacks before getting in your sleeping bag.
- Climb in bed with every thing zipped up and snugged tight. Don't wait until the middle of the night to try and close your hood.
- Eat a big dinner. Metabolism requires calories.

99. Wear it all to bed

I have camped with other people who strip down before going to bed and then spend time in the morning putting those clothes back on. Some people even bring a special set of clothes to sleep in! (These *special* clothes are called pajamas.) That is traditional camping. You carried insulating clothes into the mountains, so use 'em! Wearing all your clothes lets you bring a lighter sleeping bag; it makes your clothes part of a complete sleeping system (see tip 21). I wear all my clothes to bed at night, yes—all of 'em. This includes a bandana around my neck, my raincoat, and my gloves. When it comes time to get up in the morning, there is no issue about being chilly; I simply get up.

I do NOT wear wet gear to bed. If it's raining, the ambient air temperature is significantly warmer than on a calm, clear night, so I don't worry about getting as cold. I keep the rain gear nearby in a soggy pile under the tarp. I don't try to "dry" my wet layers on an internal clothes line because I know (from experience) that doesn't really work.

100. The humble pillow

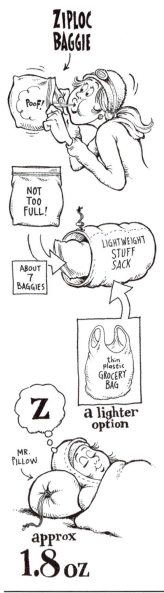

ZIPLOC BAGGIE

POOF!

NOT TOO FULL!

ABOUT 7 BAGGIES

LIGHTWEIGHT STUFF SACK

thin plastic GROCERY BAG

a lighter option

Z

MR. PILLOW

approx
1.8 oz

I love a pillow under my head during sleepy time. The traditional camper will simply take a porky jacket, cram it into some big stuff sack, and call it good.

If you are a true ultralight zealot, you'll be sleeping in a very thin sleeping bag (or quilt), and comfort dictates that you'll wear all your clothes to bed. This means there is nothing left over for your pillow.

You'll spend roughly one-third of any expedition asleep on your pad. This time is vital to your recovery and well-being. If you need a pillow to sleep well, then don't short yourself. There are plenty of tricked-out camping pillows on the market. Very few are light enough to be called UL.

Here's the simplest (and lightest) solution I've found: I'll fill a very light stuff sack with partially inflated Ziploc baggies. I blow air into them and zip them shut, and partially full is much better than beach-ball tight. I use the thinner sandwich style rather than the denser freezer bags. I have an 8×14-inch stuff sack, and I use seven baggies.

Test your "pillow" before you go into the field. I tried different baggies over multiple nights, and the weight of my big head ended up deflating them all by morning. My R&D determined that the baggies require a stout double zipper. Total pillow weight: 1.8 ounces. Replace the stuff sack with a wispy-thin plastic grocery bag for even more weight savings.

Other UL pillow options are sight dependent. I've filled my backpack with pinecones, and that was wonderful, but the only reason I could pull that off was because I found a huge pile of pinecones right near my sleep site. Sand in the backpack is very nice too; tiny pebbles ain't bad either.

101. How much water should be on your back?

Ryan Jordan, the man behind backpackinglight.com, shared a simple, no-nonsense little adage about water in the backcountry. Here goes:

If you arrive at a water source with water still on your back, you have made a mistake.

This truism is so obvious that it's hardly worth mentioning, except that in the age of 3-liter CamelBak hydration systems, it's utterly ignored.

I have watched UL nerds brag about the minuscule base weight of their pack and then load up on multiple liters of water, only to step over streams as they travel in the mountains. Yes, there are times when it is advisable to carry water, sometimes lots of it (see tip 111), but just be mindful of when it's truly appropriate.

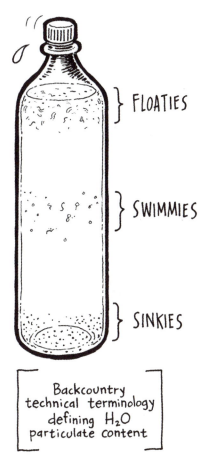

} FLOATIES

} SWIMMIES

} SINKIES

Backcountry technical terminology defining H_2O particulate content

If you can read a map, you should be able to plan out your water sources. Sometimes it's okay to carry *no water at all* if you are in an environment with lots of reliable clean running water (see tip 105).

How much do you truly need on your back? One liter of water weighs 2.2 pounds (35.2 ounces/1,000 grams), making water one of your heaviest necessities. You body requires *at the very least* 4 liters of water per day when exercising, and in extremely hot weather you'll want to drink even more. For most situations, I have vessels to handle a mere 1.5-liter capacity. In all but the driest situations, that's plenty.

I play a game when I'm hiking; it begins when I wake up in the morning and ends when I lie down to go to sleep at night. I drink as much as I can, continually throughout the day. At the same time, I try to never carry more than half a liter on my back. Sometimes I cheat by carrying the water bottle in my hand as I hike. (Wait, that's not cheating; that's smart!)

I track my hydration level by how often I need to pee, and I monitor the color of the urine. Clear is a sign of proper hydration; dark yellow is a sign that I should be drinking more.

1-liter
WATER BOTTLE
(free!)

0.8 oz

1-liter
PLATYPUS
SOFT-BOTTLE
(about $9)

0.9 oz

1-liter
SODA BOTTLE
(free!)

1.5 oz

1-liter
LEXAN BOTTLE
(about $10)

6.3 oz

102. What's the lightest tool for carrying water?

The absolutely easiest and cheapest solution for carrying water is the humble plastic bottle from the recycle bin. These come in a convoluted variety of shapes and sizes, so let the scale decide.

- A 1-liter *water* bottle (thinner plastic) weighs 0.8 ounce.
- A 1-liter *Platypus* (collapsible vessel) weighs 0.9 ounce.
- A 1-liter *soda* bottle (thicker plastic) weighs 1.5 ounces.
- A 1-liter *Nalgene Lexan* bottle weighs 6.3 ounces. (Ugh!)

If you need to carry a lot of water (see tip 111), the best option is a soft-sided collapsible Platypus, or a few of them. There is no true NEED for hydration systems with hoses and bite valves; those are WANTS.

103. Filling a water bottle

The tiny mouth on a standard soda bottle can make it almost impossible to fill in shallow little puddles. Because of that, I keep my trusty mug right at the top of my pack. When I need to fill my bottle, having that mug handy for scooping makes life a lot easier. Plus, I can monitor the floaties and sinkies (and swimmies) a little better as I pour into my bottle. A Ziploc plastic bag is a good dipping tool too.

This very simple tip is a real-deal time saver.

DON'T pour above the puddle!

impossible to dip a big bottle

Dip carefully

DON'T LOSE the CAP!

(all you need is a tiny trickle)

Water

For the really tiny puddles, this requires some subtlety. If all you have is a tiny trickle, it's easy to get murky water; the challenge is to get super-clear water. Take your time; be patient. Walk up- and downstream to find the best spot to position your mug, and be as gentle as an artist. This water will sustain your life; there's no reason to slam your mug in a puddle and drink brown glop. (See tip 112.)

IODINE
I 53
Atomic Wt. 126.9045

SNIFFFF!
very slight
chemical
odor...

slightly
BRowN
color

104. Add electrolytes when you need 'em

You'll need to continually replenish your body with salt and potassium in order to function. If you are drinking *and* eating during the day, there should be no need for anything else. But on a long hike, you are placing extra stresses on your body, so you might find some benefits to an electrolyte additive.

Currently the market is awash in a ridiculous number of sports drinks with labels dense with scientific jargon and long lists of perplexing ingredients. Be aware that some powdered additives are mostly sugar, so you are essentially drinking candy.

Whatever you take, be mindful of the weight of the packaging. Just so you know, an empty Emergen-C package weighs just under 1 gram (0.0025 ounce).

WATER TREATMENT CHART

BRAND	STYLE	CHEMICAL	TASTE	WEIGHT	SPEED	COMMENTS	OVERALL
AQUAMIRA	A&B drops	Chlorine dioxide	●●●	●●	●●●	can be pre-mixed	●●●
AQUAMIRA	tablets	Chlorine dioxide	●	●●●	●	no way to vary amount used	●
POTABLE AQUA	tablets	Iodine	●	●	●●●	must be stored in glass	●●

●●● = GooD, ●● = So So, ● = lame
All methods are very effective and have long shelf life.

105. Should you drink untreated water?

Is it safe to drink water straight from a mountain stream? The answer is an unequivocal *sometimes*.

Please be aware, drinking untreated water might have serious gastrointestinal consequences. The textbook signs and symptoms of giardia read as follows: *"Explosive diarrhea with a foul sulfurous odor."* That sounds gross, right? Knowing what is reliable in the backcountry is critical here, and making an informed decision is a combination of experience and a working knowledge of the hazards.

My pal Phil carries a cute little 500-milliliter plastic juice bottle in his hand during all his mountain travel. It's never on his back, so it adds zero to the pack weight. When he gets to a

trustworthy water source, he fills up and drinks. Nothing to treat; no pumping, no hoses, no boiling, no mixing chemicals, no time waiting for anything. Phil has achieved a sort of mastery when evaluating the safety of water, and this came from years of experience in the backcountry. I'm a little more cautious than Phil, but I regularly drink untreated water.

I realize I am outside the norm of camping practices to even suggest that it's okay to *sometimes* drink water straight from its source. It might even come off as heresy in a world filled with filters, pumps, chemicals, and weird glowing ultraviolet battery-operated gizmos. These tools serve a purpose, but not all the time. In my opinion, it is entirely appropriate to do what we as humans have done since the dawn of time.

I drink only from springs and very small streams. And I've found that a lot of the small streams are easy to follow uphill to their source, where the water bubbles up out of the ground. This is actually very easy to do, especially with a UL pack. If you are aware, and looking uphill, you'll quickly gain a good sense of where to find the quality springs. Before drinking directly from any untreated water source, I run through this simple checklist:

SAFE WATER CHECKLIST:

☐ Are there any zones above this water source that could impact the quality (popular campsites, mine sites, moose mating grounds, etc.)?

☐ Is this a popular camping zone?

☐ Is the water running from an outlet of a lake or pond?

☐ Are there any wildlife feces near the water or upstream?

☐ Is there a dead elk in the stream?

If I answer NO to all these questions, I happily drink up—most of the time. I'll add that if I find a spring bubbling straight up from the ground, I will always dip my cup as close as I can to the source.

My advice: Carefully factor in all available data before drinking ANY water in the backcountry. For questionable sources, I carry Aquamira, a chlorine-based water treatment.

106. How I use Aquamira

My preferred system for treating suspect water is Aquamira. This is a chlorine dioxide chemical treatment that leaves very little noticeable taste in the water. It has a proven track record over the years, and it has a long shelf life. And for reasons I don't understand, nowhere on the bottles does it say it makes questionable water safe to drink. It is a two-bottle system of very stable A & B liquids that when mixed create a dependable solution for waterborne pathogens.

aqua mira

chlorine dioxide mix

(shown here in the OVERSIZED bottles)

3.0 oz

AQUAMIRA
repackaged in very
tiny bottles

I advocate a system that does not quite match the written directions on the bottle. Here's what I do for myself:

• I repackage the A & B into two smaller bottles, using a Sharpie to clearly label each of these tiny bottles.

• The system requires a third bottle that gets labeled Mix. I'll use the smallest (black or opaque) bottle I can for this purpose. The reason for the smallest bottle is that I don't want to store this mix for too long; I want to use it up well before it has a chance to lose its effectiveness.

• Before hiking in the morning, I premix an equal amount of A and B liquid into the tiny Mix bottle. The tiny bottle I use will hold only about 40 drops total, so I use 20 drops of A and 20 of B.

• I usually carry this premix in my pocket and use it to treat my water each time I refill my bottle during the day. All my teammates use my drops too. No need to stop and wait; just dip, drop, and go.

- I err on the side of caution and add a little more time to the suggested amount in the instructions. I hike with my treated water for at least twenty minutes before taking my first sip.
- I carefully monitor the color of the liquid that comes out of the bottle marked Mix to make sure it has a bright yellow tone. If the drops come out clear, the mix has lost its effectiveness; I squeeze it all out and start over.
- The effectiveness of the premix is severely compromised by temperature, sunlight, and time. Temperature is hard to control if you are in a hot environment. Sunlight is easier; simply keep the vessel inside your pack (or pocket), and don't use a clear-plastic bottle.

How Many Drops?

The instructions say to use 7 drops each of A and B for 1 liter of water. That means, if you want to follow the instructions exactly, you'll need a total of 14 drops of the mix to treat 1 liter of water. Before we proceed further, those instructions were written by lawyers! So let's factor that into the equations.

I try and temper those instructions with a little judgment. I use as little as I feel necessary. For a reliable water source, I won't treat at all; I'll just drink it untreated. But that's just me (see tip 105). If you get water from a glacier-fed stream in the mountains in Alaska, the need for following the exact instructions is slight. But if I get water from a lake in the Tetons that has an impacted campsite nearby, I'll use 7 drops of the mix for about 1 liter of water—approximately half of what the directions recommend.

Maybe I'll use a little more if there are multiple campsites around the lake. And if there are piles of sheep droppings all around that same lake, I'll follow the instructions exactly, using all 14 drops. No good answer here, and if you get sick, don't sue me!

How Long Will the Premix Last?

Time is a judgment call, and I simply can't give a decisive answer. If the mixture is bright yellow, it is presumed to be effective. The yellow will slowly disappear over time. Because I use a very tiny bottle for the premix, it's usually used up within twenty-four hours. The tiny bottle is a simple bit of insurance.

If it's hot and sunny, I wouldn't use the premix after twenty-four hours. In moderate conditions, I feel that three days is too long, but forty-eight hours seems a conservative amount of time to trust its effectiveness in cool weather.

It's impossible to truly know the quality of the premix. When in doubt, simply err on the side of caution by dumping it out.

If I am even slightly concerned the solution might be old or compromised, I start over.

107. Don't stop hiking just because it's raining

Alas, it's not as nice as hiking on a beautiful sunny day. But be assured, you won't melt. There are a multitude of tiny tricks that can keep you comfortable in rainy weather.

Hiking in the rain means two things are happening: It's raining on the outside, and at the same time you are wearing sweaty waterproof layers that can be wet on the inside. Make sure to minimize the next-to-skin wetness by wearing as few layers as possible. You have minimal gear as it is, so save something dry for sleeping.

Use your trail time to mentally plan out your tarp-pitching procedure in your head. By visualizing a plan ahead of time, you can avoid having to fumble too much.

- Keep your primary insulation layers (like a down coat) well waterproofed in your pack.
- Keep moving rather than taking breaks; slow down if needed.
- Monitor your speed so that you are warm but don't get sweaty.
- Let your oversized raincoat sleeves cover your hands.
- Wear glove liners; these insulate even when wet.
- Expect your feet to get soaked.
- Don't complain (it won't help).

Once your stuff gets wet, make sure to use any break in the storm to dry gear out. This ritual is referred to as a drying party, and the optimal way to dry clothes is to simply wear them. I might spend the first few hours of a post-rain sun event hiking with all my wet gear. I'll hike nice and slow, and everything will be unzipped.

DRYING
the damp
SLEEPING BAG
in the
morning

If the down sleeping bag is damp in the morning, I might strap it to the top of my pack while I hike. I'll make sure to secure it really well; it's too valuable to have fall in the mud because I was too lazy to do a good job.

108. Waterproof your gear

I do NOT use a pack cover. They don't actually cover the entire pack, so they don't truly protect the contents from rain. I like to waterproof my gear so that absolutely everything will stay perfectly dry even if my pack falls in a river and floats downstream, taking me all day to catch it again. I line my backpack with ONE trash compactor bag.

Hefty trash compactor bag

18-gallon (68-liter) size

25¾×35 inches/2.5 millimeters thick

Cost: less than a buck per bag

These are heavy-gauge white plastic bags designed for kitchen trash compactors. I have never found anything better or lighter. They are white, so it's easy to find stuff deep in the bag. Plus, they are tough enough to last for multiple trips.

They weigh 2.2 ounces and are plenty big to line the entirety of my backpack. There is enough extra left over on top to twirl around into a snout (lovingly called the elephant's snout), and this gets tucked snugly into the side of the pack (pointing downward) for absolute waterproofing. I'm very careful not to poke holes in this bag (see tip 26); I have no redundancy.

If the tarp is wet in the morning, I stuff it in the bottom of my backpack FIRST and then put the compactor bag on top. Wet and dry stuff are separated, and everything stays dry INSIDE the compactor bag.

I put my rain gear on top, outside the compactor bag, because if it rains, I'll end up wearing it. Simple!

WHITE PLASTIC COMPACTOR BAG

WATER-PROOF LINER goes in NEXT

the WET TARP goes in FIRST

The TARP gets pushed to the BOTTOM

SOGGY-STUFF stays separate from the dry gear

TWIRL nice & tight (the elephant snout!)

the snout GETS TUCKED IN!

WATERPROOFING the PACK

109. How to dry wet socks

Thick traditional wool hiking socks take a long time to dry. Thinny-thin shorty-short synthetic socks (see tip 85) dry super fast. You can expedite any wet sock issues by taking the most efficient gear.

My favorite system for drying wet socks is to wring 'em out first and then put them in my pockets when I'm traveling. Most hiking-specific pants (and shorts) are equipped with mesh fabric in the pockets. These, combined with body heat and the walking motions, will dry the socks out efficiently.

Some backpacks have mesh pockets. These work okay for drying wet gear, but things stay scrunched and compressed, so expect the process to be slow.

Sloppy hikers simply drape their socks on some strap on their pack as they travel. This is a sure-fire way to lose an important piece of gear. (See tip 27.) If you do attach something to your pack, just make darn sure it's truly attached. Tie it in a knot, or clip something through something else.

110. Rain skirts: the functional fashion statement

Gravity goes straight down, so my legs get protected (mostly) from the falling rain by this very fashionable item. It has plenty of breathability, and I can wear it if I sit on wet ground. This

THE RAIN SKIRT
(make yer own, it's easy)

---

is a very easy make-it-yourself item, and the results are both functional and stylish. I've made a series of these, and none weighs more than 2 ounces!

The instructional cartoon doesn't show a sewing machine. But if you are even a mediocre seamstress (see tip 22), it's easy to create something nice. The pants that come with DriDucks and Frogg Toggs rain outfits are easy to modify using scissors and masking tape!

111. Desert travel skills

The desert may seem like a barren wasteland, but it can be a place of deep and mysterious rewards. By definition, a desert is a place of extreme dryness. Prickly plants and a few little lizards have evolved to deal with an almost complete absence of water, but we have not.

Your needs in a hot desert environment can be summed up with these three points: water, water, and water. If you solve these needs, everything else should be easy.

I've stated that it's okay to travel without water in your pack (see tip 101), but this only applies to places with plentiful water sources. In the desert you might be required to carry a lot of water, potentially gallons. The best UL tool I've found for hauling big water loads is Platypus-style water bottles. Once empty, they fold up small, and they come in sizes up to 3 liters.

How much water do you truly need? No good answer, but 5 liters a day (well over a gallon) per person in hot weather is the bare minimum. And the desert is a place where some electrolyte replacement additive will serve a very real purpose (see tip 104).

This is an environment of extremes, with blistering hot days separated by bitter cold nights. Don't short yourself on warm clothes in a place where you'll need them only after the sun goes down.

Early morning and evening can be exceptionally beautiful in the desert; the middle of the day can be brutal. Plan for nap time in the shade (see tip 72) during the hottest hours.

112. Make the most of desert water sources

There is water in the desert, just not a lot. Plan your route around known and dependable water. This information is out there—do your research before heading off into the sand and rocks.

A "reliable" water source might be nothing more than a murky brown puddle, but it's still water. A traditional camper would filter it with a mechanical pump (which would probably clog), but the UL hiker can solve the problem with much lighter gear. The water can be filtered using a bandana or mosquito head net. A simple plastic kitchen funnel (0.5 ounces) helps the process a lot. Remember to add a chemical treatment (like Aquamira) to any suspect water.

small kitchen
FUNNEL
(about ½ oz)

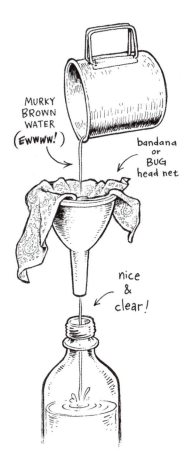

MURKY
BROWN
WATER
(EWWWW!)

bandana
or
BUG
head net

nice
&
clear!

If a bear stands upright it's probably only trying to see (and smell) you...

DON'T PANIC!

113. Camping in bear country

There are many very real concerns when traveling in grizzly or black bear territory, and these simple tips should not be considered a substitute for prudent judgment and a dose of humility. This text is simply to highlight the issues surrounding bears and ultralight backpacking.

Traveling and camping with less gear in bear country is significantly simpler. It is easier to get up to higher elevations, out of the dense trees and bear corridors that make for spooky travel and camping. The high country has the advantage of expansive views, because it's much more difficult to surprise a bear in open terrain.

The traditional heavy backpack creates an oppressive need to camp wherever you wind up at the end of a long day. If it's early evening and you are down in the trees, it can be a brutal decision to trudge uphill for a safer campsite. You can make a lousy choice based on your physical limitations and the heavy pack.

One very real safety concern is that the ultralight hiker can move very fast on the trail, creating a need for heightened awareness. Rounding corners on the trail in the forest while moving at a quick pace is potentially fatal in bear country. If you surprise a sow with cubs, you might be gasping your last breath in a puddle of your own blood. And the bear itself would inevitably end up dead from a ranger's rifle. Everybody loses.

GRIZZLY
Ursus arctos

BLACK BEAR
Ursus americanus

GRIZZLY BEAR

BLACK BEAR

How do you manage the hazard? First, and most important, recognize that you are *not* in a petting zoo. The first four letters of *wilderness* spell *WILD*.

Don't hike alone in bear country, and stay really close to your teammates in any zones that seem even remotely suspect for hidden bears. This is less of an issue in the treeless high country, where you can spread out a little. Make noise, talk, sing, and occasionally shout, making sure there is enough noise to warn any bears of your presence.

114. Hang your food at night

Bears are smart. If they associate campers with free food, eventually there'll be grim consequences. Some areas with big bear populations will require the use of bear canisters. These are decidedly NON-ultralight. These rules are the direct result of uneducated, sloppy campers who ruined it for the rest of us. It is our *responsibility* to make sure we don't create more habituated bears and, in turn, more dogmatic rules.

The ultralight bear hang kit is essentially 45 feet (at the very least) of very strong string. My advice: Don't try to save weight by using a shorter length. I've made that mistake, so trust me.

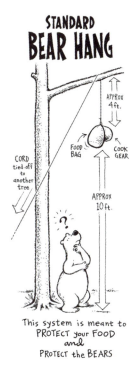

STANDARD BEAR HANG

APPROX 4 ft.

FOOD BAG

COOK GEAR

CORD tied-off to another tree

APPROX 10 ft.

?

This system is meant to PROTECT your FOOD and PROTECT the BEARS

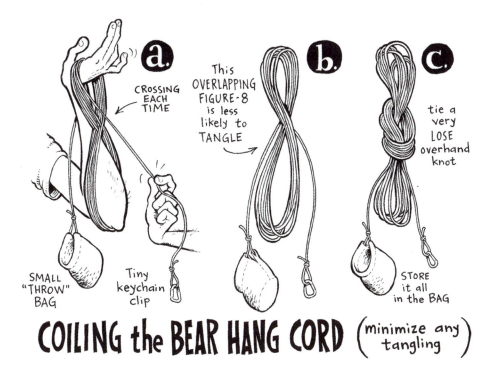

a.

CROSSING EACH TIME

This OVERLAPPING FIGURE-8 is less likely to TANGLE

SMALL "THROW" BAG

Tiny keychain clip

b.

c.

tie a very LOSE overhand knot

STORE it all in the BAG

COILING the BEAR HANG CORD (minimize any tangling)

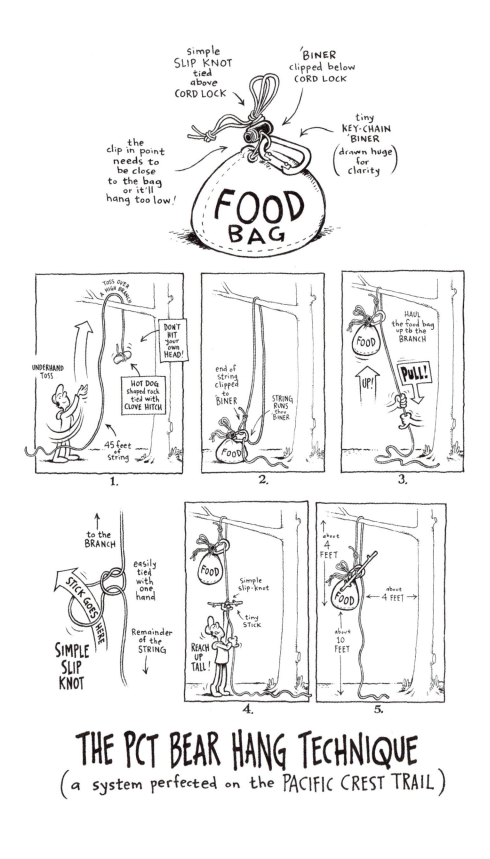

THE PCT BEAR HANG TECHNIQUE
(a system perfected on the PACIFIC CREST TRAIL)

Exceptionally strong cord is easily found on the web. Materials like Kevlar, Spectra, and urethane-coated Dyneema keep the weight down (well under 3 ounces per 50 feet) on these amazing UL cords. The drawback is that under heavy loads (like food for a team on a long trip), the thin cord can saw into a tree branch like a piano wire and get permanently stuck.

A typical bear hang kit will have:

- 45 feet of cord
- A special *throwing* stuff sack (a mesh "garlic" bag is perfect)
- A very tiny carabiner

A very basic hang involves filling the throw sack with a small rock (or even better, sand) and tossing it up and over a high branch on a tree, then clipping your food and cook gear onto the cord and hauling it up out of reach of any curious bear. Another tossing tip is to tie the string to a hot dog–shaped rock using a clove hitch.

For more advanced hanging techniques, precautions, and facts please see both *Allen & Mike's Really Cool Backpackin' Book* and *Lighten Up!*

115. Keep the bear spray handy

I have two friends who have been mauled by grizzly bears. Both tell a chilling story where the actual attack happened so fast that they had no time to react.

Always carry bear spray in bear country! Keep this 12.2-ounce can in a holster within easy reach on your hip belt.

Here's one thing that I see all too often: Bear spray carried by hikers in real-deal bear terrain that's clipped with a carabiner on the BACK of their pack or, worse yet, stowed INSIDE the pack, rendering it utterly useless when it's needed. This stuff needs to be deployed in nanoseconds! Those wand pockets on the side of a pack are a poor choice too. A holster on the hip

BE CAREFUL!

REMOVABLE TRIGGER GUARD

BEAR PEPPER SPRAY

little String 'cuz You don't wanna lose the trigger guard!

STRETCHY FABRIC

HOLSTER

BELT THINGY

12.2 oz total

PFFT!

PEPPER SPRAY DEFENSE

belt is second only to actually holding it in your hand. The stuff inside is dangerous. It's a powerful pepper aerosol, and the can should be treated with the utmost respect.

For more detailed safety info, read *Allen and Mike's Really Cool Backpackin' Book.*

116. Liberate yourself from toilet paper

I'm always disappointed when my camping teammates walk into the woods for a dump run and bring along their toilet paper (TP). Good grief, what kind of wilderness experience is that? Mankind has been pooping in the woods since we climbed down out of the trees, and TP is a pretty recent invention when you look at human history.

We live in a society with user-friendly toilets, and they all come equipped with a wonderful roll of TP. There's nothing for us to think about; we do our duty, wipe, and flush. We've created a very nice convenience, but it has separated us from what should be a very simple bit of outdoor know-how.

Why are so many campers so dependent on toilet paper? I would have to guess that they've never in their life used anything other than the store-bought stuff on a roll. Or they've had a bad experience with their one and only time with natural wiping material. It's a sad truth: Natural butt wiping is a lost art.

Too many people bury their used TP or, worse, just leave it on the surface. We don't have to deal with it in the bathroom; we simply flush. Sadly, this transfers to *not dealing* in the backcountry too. It's left as trash out of an inability to *deal*.

The ultralight benefits? Not carrying TP obviously saves 100 percent of its weight. But beyond that, you are liberated from something that we *think* we need.

Over the decades I have found an awful lot of used toilet paper in the mountains, and it's disgusting. (See tip 44.) My heart sinks every time. Finding used toilet paper leaves me absolutely disgusted at all humanity. I deal with these piles of white (and brown) toilet paper. I carry it out, and I don't shy away from this thankless chore. Am I a weirdo zealot about not using toilet paper? Sure enough, but it wells up from dealing with other people's laziness.

If you do bring store-bought toilet paper, I feel strongly that it must be carried out and not just left in the backcountry (for me to find). Triple-bag it before it goes back in your pack. Burning is not recommended; this is an all too common cause of forest fires.

SNOW for WIPING

① the
BARE HANDED METHOD:
grab a handfull of soft snow...

② SQUEEZE!

③ VOI-LA!
"Toilet paper"
with a nice
wiping point...

NOTICE: This technique
din't gunna work too well with
cold, dry, non-cohesive snow!
good luck!

WHAT TO USE?

The backcountry is home to a plentitude of wonderful wiping things. Any camper who wants to make fun of natural TP will immediately sneer and mention pinecones. Yes, just the image of a pinecone with all those pointy things makes my butt wince. With very few exceptions, pinecones do NOT work! But if you find a batch from a Douglas fir, you've got the goods!

soft & papery

DOUGLAS FIR CONE

SNOW

If you have snow available, you will have a stupendously clean bunghole! No foolin'—snow has all the properties that make it the crème de la crème of natural butt wiping. Snow is the perfect combo of smooth and abrasive, it's just wet enough for a little extra cleaning power, and it's white! The whiteness will allow the wiper to accurately monitor any residue in the area in question. Plus, if you have snow, you usually have a LOT of it.

Don't use gloves; use your bare hand and make a snowball by squeezing. Don't make a round snowball shape; you want to create a pointy feature for the business end.

Here's an insight into my personal wiping habits: I use a LOT of wiping material. I am never satisfied until I know that things are super-*duper*-clean. I encourage you to strive for the same high standards.

RIVER ROCKS

Smooth and elegant, these polished beauties are the second best behind snow. Before visiting your private zone, collect a load of these rocks. Not too big, not too small, a little flat, a little pointy, and definitely NOT round. Once again, grab a lot of 'em.

tiny stone

too small.

BIG Rock!

too big!

luxuriously smooth River Rock!

just right!

ROCKS as T.P.

LEAVES

For the most part, leaves don't work; they can be thin and easily torn. If you do use little leaves, use a small stack of them so that your finger tip doesn't poke through at the wrong moment. I've had better luck using the back side of leaves, where the raised veins can act as little scrubbers.

Not all leaves are below par. Most of the Northern Hemisphere has been graced with a gangly weed called mullein (*Verbascum thapsus),* and a very similar plant called woolly lamb's ear (*Stachys byzantina*). These are both rather homely plants, but the leaves are like the wings of an angel. They are big, thick, strong, fuzzy, and satisfying. These plants are pretty common, and they grow in clumps. If you are collecting these leaves, please carefully get them from multiple plants, taking just a few leaves from each. Do not strip one of these cute fuzzy plants of all its leaves just to guarantee yourself a tidy butt. You don't need to kill anything for hygiene!

SMOOTH STICKS

A downed tree with dry, weathered branches can be wonderful. Look for a collection of sticks about 1 inch in diameter, with minimal poking protuberances. Pick the smoothest side for wiping, taking advantage of the long, featureless length of the stick.

OLD MAN'S BEARD

Have you ever marveled at that weird electric-yellow moss that hangs from pine trees? This stuff is great. Once again, grab a little bit from multiple trees.

GRASS

A goodly clump of grass makes for a pretty good cleaning tool. For a nice stiff set of bristles, you can fold the grass into a very tidy little brush. Grab the grass from a big zone; avoid stripping an area of all its green stuff.

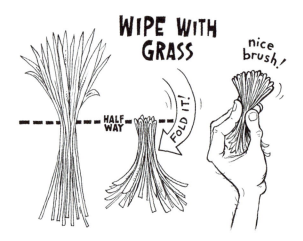

SIZE REQUIRED

For obvious reasons, you'll want to keep your hands away from the contaminants you're trying to wipe away. Whatever you use, make sure it's big enough to keep your fingers a good distance from the working area.

THE BUTT SCUFF ON DEWY TUFTS OF GRASS

Sometimes you are in an environment with tufts of grass that look like little fright wigs. These usually come in groups, and on a calm dewy morning, there is nothing more wonderful in the world. You can sit on one of these like a bicycle seat and slide yourself along, letting the tuft do its scouring duty. If you find a row of these, get ready to cry tears of joy. And if

you have a little bit of downhill slope to work with, the job is a lot easier.

PLAN AHEAD AND PREPARE

Before the urge becomes a raging alarm, there are a few small things you'll need to do. The act of collecting the wiping tools may take a little time and some searching. Start planning well before the need arises. Begin filling your pockets with lots of nice smooth rocks (or leaves, sticks, etc.). Keep an eye out for the perfect collection of broad leaf plants. Is it a short walk to a patch of snow still unmelted from last winter?

Do not–I repeat–DO NOT just squat down and expect to find the perfect wiping material within arm's reach. It won't be there; I know from experience. No need to describe this unpleasant dilemma.

THE CAT HOLE

You will need to dig a shallow hole, and the UL tool of choice is a tent stake. The thin wire stakes won't work; you'll need at least one stake that is a little stouter. A trekking pole is a good tool too; just make sure to hold it low near the pointy end while digging. Other options are a sharp stick or a pointy rock.

The recommended technique espoused by wilderness authorities is to take a trowel and dig a 6- to 8-inch-deep hole. This is easy to draw (I know, I've drawn it in multiple books), but it can be hard to actually *do*. There are a lot of places where the ground is too hard and it simply will not work, even with the best metal trowel. In some environments the soil is too rocky (or too dense) to get down that deep. If you can't dig down deep enough, go wider, or create a shallow trench. No good answer here; my advice is to do the *very best job you can do,* whatever the circumstances.

The goal is to get the fecal matter to decompose in the organic soil near the surface. The microorganisms will do their job and eventually change the dubious properties into something sterile. How long this might take is hard to say, but it will happen a lot faster in rich, living topsoil. It will happen exceedingly slow on the surface or under rocks. Please understand; there is the very real potential to contaminate water sources with human feces, so the simple act of properly burying your waste is a necessary undertaking.

After the bomb is dropped in the hole, take a little time to stir it up and mix it well with the organic soil. Yes, this basically means you get to play with your own poop. This important stirring process can dramatically accelerate the decomposition time. Please use a stick and not the tent stake.

At the end, refill the hole and cover the ground in a way that will disguise your job site. Take pride in this step; it will allow future visitors a pristine visual experience.

WHAT TO DO WITH THE USED MATERIAL?
After wiping you'll need to dispose of the natural toilet paper. If you've dug a deep enough hole, depositing the wipers in

there is a great solution. Refill the hole, and you're done. But sometimes you can only get the first few wipers in the hole because it's too full (or barely deep enough), so you'll have to toss the rest. Carefully look around for a good place to deliver the contaminated post-wipe product. Avoid any spot where a fellow camper may travel or step, and think about where water will run in the rain. Under a big bush is a good solution.

HYGIENE

Wash your hands when you're done. This is a vital part of the whole process. Don't be a slob—fecal contamination is the cause of backcountry NVD! That's nausea, vomiting, and diarrhea!

For the highest degree of success, employ your teammate as a helper. When you come back from your dump run, tell them that you'll require their assistance. They can dig through the pack (let them touch things with clean hands), getting the soap and a water bottle. They put the soap in your hands, and they pour the water. Your contaminated hands touch nothing.

HYGIENE TOOLS

I always carry soap and alcohol hand-sanitizing gel, both repackaged in tiny dropper bottles. These are essential safety

components in my backcountry kit of dinky things. For soap, I am a devotee of Dr. Bronner's; almond is my favorite.

TIME REQUIRED

The humble act of pooping in the woods involves a goodly amount of busywork. You need to collect the wiping material, find a private spot, dig a cat hole, fill it, wipe effectively, stir the poop, fill the hole back in, disguise the little area, and wash your hands. Plus you need to do a good job on each of these important steps.

If your partner says it's dump time and then comes back after just a minute, do NOT let 'em put their hand in your bag of gorp! Doing a good job requires at least ten minutes.

117. Clean your butt!

A fellow backcountry traveler once spoke this little truism: "A clean butt is a happy butt!" Words to live by.

On a long trip, taking a little time to wash your butt is essential to your wilderness experience. This humble act can genuinely make the world a more wonderful place. I've taken pride in teaching this valuable skill, and my students truly enjoy the benefits.

Find a private spot away from the trail and away from any running water. You'll need at least 1 liter of water in a bottle and some kind of soap. A nice warm day makes this all the more pleasant. Pants off and squat down. The area getting washed will be positioned low, so gravity will ensure that all the water should run off onto the ground. Dedicate one hand for doing all the *clean* work (right), and the other hand for doing all the *dirty* work (left). The right hand opens the water bottle and squeezes the little soap vial, never touching the left. Just a tiny bit of soap is plenty. The left hand rubs and scrubs. C'mon, get right in there and do a high-quality job!

Here's a rinse trick: In the squatty pose, you can pour water along your left arm with your right hand, the water will run like a sluice, and gravity will deliver it down into that workzone. This rinsing works perfectly. The other option is to reach around behind yourself and pour water down your lower back, positioning the bottle at the base of your spine. When the washing is done and the soap is rinsed off, the pants come up.

Then wash your hands, and do a good job! Really rub those hands together. This scrubbing action is essential—don't be lazy. And point your fingers downward so that gravity will let the water and soap (and those germs too) fall off and onto the ground. If you fingers are pointed up, everything runs down along your arms and into your sleeves.

Give a good rinse with nonsoapy water. The final step involves antibacterial alcohol gel; just a little and you're done.

I do NOT use a hanky or a washcloth for washing anything "private" in the backcountry; it's just too hard to clean completely.

I know plenty of backcountry comrades who use this soap-and-water washing method every single time they poop in the woods. This technique will guarantee a sparkling orifice—and a *very* happy camper.

118. Stoves and cooking—keep it light!

I've monkeyed with a lot of camping stoves over the decades. Butane canisters are heavy, expensive, and hard to recycle. White gas needs an expensive and heavy stove, plus it requires a metal fuel bottle. No need to acknowledge these non-UL options.

My favorite ultralight solution is using alcohol fuel to heat water. It has a little bit slower boil time than a traditional backpacker's stove, but everything about it is simple. There are no moving parts to break, and the alcohol can be carried in a plastic soda bottle.

When I say alcohol, I mean *denatured alcohol* from the hardware store. As a fuel source, it's cheap and simple, but it won't pump out comparable BTUs to a traditional white gas contraption. Alcohol stoves are for summertime only; don't try to use an alcohol stove in the Himalayas in winter!

An efficient alcohol stove setup requires:

- A stove
- A pot or mug (with a lid)
- A windscreen
- Sometimes a stand (easily made using three tent stakes)

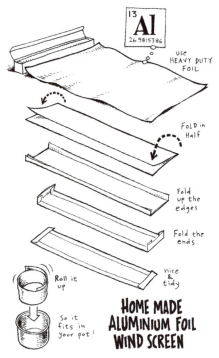

use
HEAVY DUTY
FOIL

FoLD in
Half

Fold
up the
edges

Fold the
ends

nice
&
tidy

Roll it
up

So it
fits in
your pot!

HOME MADE ALUMINIUM FOIL WIND SCREEN

Alcohol stoves don't have a shut-off valve; you just fill the reservoir and let it burn till it's all gone. I've found that you can get really good at estimating the volume of fuel needed; just peek in the stove as you pour the fuel and make a good guess. Most stoves are so tiny that you can't really waste fuel because they just don't hold that much.

The pot lid is a vital tool to maximize the efficiency of the boil time, but you don't need to use the (heavy) lid that came with the pot. For a substantial weight savings, you can make a lid from an old pie pan or folded-over aluminum foil. Keep the lid snug with a little rock.

The foil lid is very light, and I take one on weekend trips. But on a longer trip, the added efficiency of using the actual lid will make up its weight in saved fuel. A nice tight-fitting lid will expedite cozy cooking too.

Heavy-duty kitchen aluminum foil is just fine for a windscreen. Size the screen so that it rolls up and fits neatly inside the pot for carrying.

If the pot doesn't have a handle, you'll need a way to lift it off the flame. You can use a standard aluminum pot lifter, which should weigh around 1 ounce. Some folks just use a gloved hand, but I've seen wool gloves get toasted and synthetic gloves melt!

One concern is that alcohol is an almost perfectly silent fuel, so you may not know when the stove has gone out and needs a little more fuel.

At night the flame from alcohol burns with a mysterious blue glow, but it is almost completely invisible during daylight. Be super cautious when dealing with a lit stove. It is very easy to burn yourself or your clothing. It's all too

MELTING
FABRIC!

INVISIBLE
FLAME!

alcohol stove

Stoves

common to melt the fabric of your wind shirt on the underside of your wrist.

And most important, *do not add more liquid alcohol to a lit stove!* Trust me on this one; it's a really bad idea. I speak from experience.

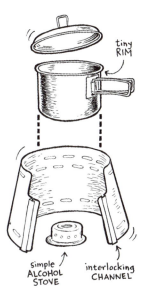

simple
ALCOHOL
STOVE

interlocking
CHANNEL

A simple homemade alcohol stove works beautifully for solo and two-person cook teams. But once you get up to three people cooking with one stove, you'll find the limitations of these little beauties. For three people you'll be happier with a more robust alcohol stove, and that means the beautiful Trangia from Sweden. Sporting an all-brass construction and a tried-and-true design, this unit is sort of heavy (3.2 ounces), but it can really crank out the heat for three hungry campers.

Another system for maximizing efficiency is the amazing Caldera Cone system. This is a combination windscreen and stove stand that supports the pot above the stove. The cone is ordered in a size that will match your specific cook pot. The weight of the cone is quickly offset by the fuel saved, even on a short trip. Highly recommended.

119. What size pot do you need?

The sizes noted below are about as small (and light) as you could go for convenience. I've played around with each of these configurations solo, as well as in big teams.

~ 1 person—500-milliliter cup

~ 2 people—1-liter pot

~ 3 people—1.3-liter pot (with a Trangia stove)

~ 4 people—Two separate two-person cook teams

120. Make your own alcohol stove

(all set up)

**CALDERA CONE
STOVE SYSTEM**

There are oodles of cool designs for homemade alcohol stoves, and they are all made from junk out of the recycle bin. Searching the Internet for alcohol stove designs is like going down the rabbit hole; be prepared to get overwhelmed with information. The stove designs drawn here are made with cat food cans (see tip 4) and a simple paper punch.

For solo cooking, most stove designs require setting the pot right on the stove unit, so there is no reason for any kind of stand. The smaller size Fancy Feast cat food can stove and a solo cook mug make for an amazingly simple and efficient cook system. I was turned on to this tiny stove by Ultralight superstar Andrew Skurka. He's traveled thousands of miles with just this little beauty in his pack—no need for anything more.

3 ⅜"
CAT FOOD CAN

about a
ONE INCH
gap

THREE TENT STAKES as ALCOHOL STOVE STAND

←—2⅛"—→

FANCY FEAST
Cat food can
(SOLO)
approx 32 holes

←—3⅜"—→

5.5 oz cat food can
(larger cook pot)
approx 26 holes

If you are cooking in a team of two, the larger can (3⅜-inch diameter) requires a little gap between the stove and the bottom of the pot. You can use three tent stakes to make a perfectly sturdy platform—and get multiuse points for the stakes!

121. Calculate your alcohol fuel needs

The weight of the fuel needs to be scrutinized just like everything else in the pack. Alcohol can be stored in any ol' plastic soda bottle. Be aware that it is hard to pour when the bottle is full. The properties of the fluid are different than water, and it tends to drip down the underside of the bottle, getting your hand wet. The humble squirt lid (pilfered from a hot sauce bottle) is an excellent solution.

There is a logic to carrying a buffer, and I'll carry Esbit tabs (see tip 123) as a backup in case I run out of alcohol.

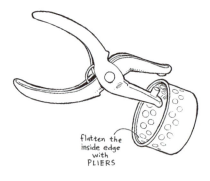

flatten the
inside edge
with
PLIERS

Alcohol weighs 27.4 ounces per liter, 78 percent the weight of water.

Warm weather calculations:

0.06 liter of fuel per person per day (good math for calm summer environments)

0.06 liter X 10 days = 0.6 liter carried as a consumable on Day 1

0.6 liter of fuel weighs 16.4 ounces

Cool weather calculations:

0.075 liter of fuel per person per day (good math for colder weather, like summer in Alaska)

0.075 liter X 10 days = 0.75 liter carried as a consumable on Day 1

0.75 liter of fuel weighs 20.6 ounces

fits a standard plastic soda bottle

PERFECT
for pouring alcohol

122. Minimize your stove's impact

Alcohol stoves are hot, and they can scorch the ground, creating a small area of sterilized topsoil. This is easy to solve, and it is an important part of leaving your cook spot as pristine as when you found it. I'll add that it is easy to start a forest fire with a camp stove. If it is excessively dry, windy, or the fire danger is rated high, please be extra careful.

Some traditional campers take an extra piece of gear (usually a sheet of metal) and place it under their stove. This works well to minimize the impact of the flame. The UL camper will use his brain, not an extra tool.

Simple solutions:

- Find some mineral soil (basically sand and pebbles free of organic duff) and create a level surface on the forest floor; less than 1 inch is plenty. After you are done with the stove, simply scatter this tiny pile so that others won't find your cook site.

- Cook on sterile, sandy soil. You'll find this kind of surface along big rivers and in high alpine environments. If the surface is sterile, there should be no concerns. I do NOT advocate cooking directly on flat sandstone in the desert Southwest; the scar may last for decades, impacting the experience of others.

- If you are cooking in a grassy environment, pour some water on the ground before you start cooking. If you are cooking near a water source, this is an easy solution.

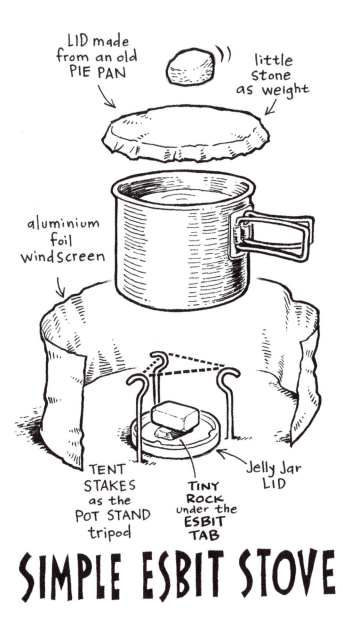

LID made from an old PIE PAN

little stone as weight

aluminium foil windscreen

TENT STAKES as the POT STAND tripod

TINY ROCK under the ESBIT TAB

Jelly Jar LID

SIMPLE ESBIT STOVE

123. The humble Esbit tab

I like these little guys, and ounce for ounce, they are the light-est fuel for boiling a small amount of water. Easy, efficient, and sort of weird, they may look a lot like sugar cubes, but don't put them in your tea!

At first I had a hard time judging how many to use for certain volumes of water, but it was an easy learning curve. I'll still use these on super short trips. Plus, they are a reliable emergency fire starter. A drawback is that they smell funny, and they can make your pack smell funny too. Triple-bag them, or use an odor-proof Ziploc-style sack. They also leave a black residue on the bottom of your pot.

0.54 oz.
(15.3 g)

THE
LIGHTEST
FUEL!

- Active ingredient: hexamethylenetetramine
- Weight per tab: 0.54 ounce (with packaging)
- Burn temperature: approximately 4,000 degrees Fahrenheit
- Burn time: approximately 12 minutes
- 1 tab brings 0.5 liter of water to a rolling boil in approximately 7 minutes
- It usually requires one and a half tabs to bring a full liter to a boil. Tabs can be cut in half using a sharp rock.

124. Woodburning stoves mean no fuel weight

There are some pretty cool options that completely eliminate the need to carry fuel. I've played with some very simple wood-burning stoves, and I really dig the concept. But the trade-off is a little extra time and a little extra soot. Neither is a big deal, but it does add some additional hassle to your day.

Plan on a messy system, and take along a plastic grocery bag to carry the stove and pot in your pack. The bag is helpful because the stove itself can get rather sooty.

If it looks like its going to rain, start collecting some dry twigs and put them in a plastic bag BEFORE it starts to rain. This is an easy solution, rather than searching for dry tinder when everything is damp.

125. The tried & true mini-BIC

This cute bit of design perfection is a scant 2 inches tall and weighs only 0.4 ounce. Not to be confused with the standard (porky) 3-inch version. They are easy to find for less than a buck at any gas station. Get a bright color (yellow or orange) so that you don't lose it in a campsite kitchen.

SOOTY
BOTTOM

FEEDING
LITTLE STICKS

AIR
VENTS

WOODBURNING STOVE

Some folks say don't take a lighter because it won't work if it gets wet. The solution is easy: Don't let it get wet! (See tip 26.) Actually, it WILL work if it gets wet; it just needs to dry out first. Put a wet lighter in an inside pocket that is mostly dry (if you are soaked on a rainy day, this might be tricky) and point the top downward while it's in there. It'll dry eventually.

Most important, remove that CHILDPROOF thingy! This extra tab of metal makes it hard to get the thing to light, especially with cold hands. Get a pair of needle-nose pliers and follow the illustrated instructions. Put the tip of the pliers in the hole where the flame comes out. Pinch the end of the itty-bitty tab that covers the roller, and yank it out! All this will make sense when you carefully inspect your lighter. Use the pliers to bend back the itty-bitty prongs that get pried upward during this modification.

126. Advanced lighting techniques

If you want to light a cigarette with the mini BIC, use your thumb. But if you want to light an alcohol stove, use your INDEX FINGER. This may seem a bit silly, but there is an advantage. If you use your thumb, your hand is pretty much a fist;

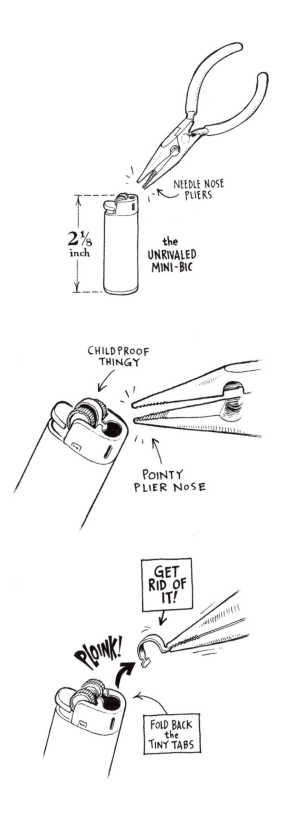

NEEDLE NOSE PLIERS

2 1/8 inch

the UNRIVALED MINI-BIC

CHILDPROOF THINGY

POINTY PLIER NOSE

GET RID OF IT!

PLOINK!

FOLD BACK the TINY TABS

Ahhhh... INDEX FINGER

simple alcohol stove

THUMB!

OW!

another
simple alcohol stove

it's hard to get that ham-shaped mass into the stove, something that might flare up.

By using your index finger, your hand is poised as an elegant artist, able to reach out sideways so that the flame is at the absolute apex of your fingers. You'll have achieved something beautiful.

Here's another trick to avoid burned fingertips: After you've filled your little stove with alcohol, just find a tiny dry stick maybe 4 inches long. Dip one end into the alcohol, pull it out, and light the soggy tip. Now you can dip that lit tip back in the stove. Make sure the flame is out before tossing the tiny stick away. Easy!

You can do the same thing with your own fingertip (really).

127. Carry a redundant fire starter

Redundant? Beware; this is the vocabulary of the traditional camper! Anytime you hear that word, you should be suspicious. However, there might be a very few items that if lost or damaged would severely impact your experience and might even make things unsafe. A fire starter is a pretty important tool.

cute
DIME
BAG

PAPER BOOK of MATCHES
0.1 oz
with baggie

If you do take a backup item, make sure it is the lightest possible solution, because in all likelihood, you won't even use it. The absolute lightest tool (and by far the cheapest!) for starting a fire is a simple paper book of twenty matches (weight 0.1 ounce); put them in a tiny plastic bag and you are done. These qualify as emergency gear.

For starting an emergency fire, I would employ a little alcohol fuel, or maybe an Esbit tab, as backup insurance. (See tip 123.)

128. Kitchen cleanup

I do NOT carry a special scrubby or sponge to clean my cook-ware; I don't use soap either. I simply use my fingers and water. I am, by definition, a professional camper, and I will not tolerate laziness in my kitchen. Be assured that my cook gear is always squeaky clean!

Here's my cleaning regimen: My backcountry meals culminate in a few extra minutes of fastidious spoon scraping. I get every delicious morsel out of the pot and mugs, and I eat it! So when it's time for the final cleanup, there should be very little left to do.

Fingertips work fine for cleaning kitchen stuff...

I perform my actual dishwashing well away from any water source so as not to contaminate a stream or lake (see tip 44) and simply rub the interior of the pot with my fingers and wipe away the last remaining microparticulates. I then scatter this cloudy water by flinging the contents on the ground. I don't pour this gray water out in one spot. There is a concern this would concentrate food smells that might attract and habituate animals.

If you had something oily in the pot, cold mountain water and fingers will still work, but it takes a few extra rounds of water and rubbing.

If something is burnt or stuck, I'll use some sand and water in the pot to scrub the sticky stuff away. And if there is snow around, the cleanup becomes super easy!

Here's a helpful hint: If you are in a team, only add oily things (like sauces or cheese) in your personal eating mugs and NOT in the bigger cook pot. This way, there is one less oily thing to clean.

129. Turkish and cowboy coffee

This is an easy way to make exceptionally wonderful coffee in the backcountry, and it's UL groovy. It is a combo of Turkish and cowboy styles, integrating the best of each technique. This system factors in my impatience, so it works well for me.

TURKISH COFFEE
made in the cup

The sludge settles to the bottom

CAUTION:

DON'T TAKE THAT LAST SIP!

THE TURKISH SOLO CUP OF GOODNESS

A. Start with the actual coffee beans. Use the inkiest and oiliest beans you can find, either French roast or espresso roast.

B. Grind the beans as fine as you possibly can. A specialty coffee shop will accommodate your needs. Most grocery stores provide a burr-style grinder, which will have a Turkish setting at the farthest end of the dial. The ground coffee should end up looking like chocolate cake flour.

C. Pack the coffee in two bags, one inside the other. The aroma is so overpowering that everything in your pack will smell like coffee if you just use a single bag.

D. In the field, bring your cup of water to a boil; take it off the heat, and pour this water into your mug.

E. Add 1 heaping spoonful of coffee to your mug and stir. The spoon itself will get stained and oily if you use it to stir, so just use the spoon to plop the coffee into your cup and then use a stick to stir.

F. Wait. How long? Hard to say. I am antsy and impatient, so this is a tricky question. Let's say less than a minute.

G. Drink. (Good, isn't it!)

H. Be careful. There is a layer of gooey stuff at the bottom of your cup, affectionately known as the sludge. No matter how tempting, *do not drink the sludge*. Trust me on this.

TURKISH
COWBOY
COFFEE
made in the
POT

POUR
VERY
SLOWLY

the grounds
settle
to the bottom

COWBOY STYLE

The tried-and-true cowboy option is good if there are *two coffee drinkers* sharing a pot.

Follow steps A through C from above.

D. Bring your pot of water to a boil. Take the pot off the heat and put it in the insulating cozy.

E. Add 2 spoonfuls of coffee to the pot; stir with a stick.

F. Wait. During the waiting time you can stir gently and tap the sides of the pot to get the fine little grounds to settle. Maybe toss a pebble in.

G. Carefully pour the coffee from the pot into the cups, being hyperaware of the sludge. The longer you wait, the less sludge. Okay, now drink.

130. Enjoy coffee on the trail

Few things are more deliriously wonderful than an afternoon snort of caffeine, especially after a nap! (See tip 72.) Brewing up hot coffee is easy enough when your cook gear is packed and ready to go in one dedicated stuff sack at the top of your pack.

There are a few forms of liquid coffee packets on the market. I recommend Java Juice, and there is a powdered single-cup version from Starbucks called VIA. These instant forms can be made hot or cold.

Cold coffee on a hot day is very easy. I carry a small baggie of powdered milk with a touch of powdered hot chocolate mixed in, affectionately called *The Mix*. In my mug goes a tiny bit of cold water (from an icy mountain spring if I can find it) and

The Mix; I add the packet of coffee last. You can avoid gloppy clumps of powdered milk by starting with minimal cold water, just a spoonful or two. I work this powder into a smooth concoction with my spoon and then add a little more water. If I'm near snow on a hot summer day, that goes in too. Drink, enjoy, repeat as necessary.

131. You CAN eat well in the backcountry

There are UL nerds who'll tinker with a razor blade, cutting every extraneous thread off their already lightweight backpack (as they should). But at the start of a trip, they'll unconsciously load that same backpack with exorbitant amounts of food.

Food requires the same scrutiny and attention to detail as any other item on your back. Consciously deliberating over your food and planning how much to carry on an expedition is a real-deal skill, just like pitching the tarp for a windy night.

I'm a good cook, and because of that I feel no need to purchase pre-made camping meals. I have the expertise and passion to make better food in my own kitchen, and this chapter reflects my dedication to homemade goodness.

Here is a deep truism: Eating food in the backcountry can be joyous.

132. Three initial steps to food planning

Step 1: Quantify all the variables.

- How long is the trip?
- How many team members are there?
- What environmental factors will influence the food needs?
- What metabolic factors will influence the food needs?

Step 2: Create a tidy data sheet, and stick to it!

Step 3: AFTER the trip is over, carefully review how it all worked. Keep exacting records about how much leftover food you came home with, what was enjoyed, and what felt unsatisfying. Use this data to fine-tune your next trip.

133. How much food do you need per day?

Food needs are figured using *pounds per person per day* (PPPPD). This simple acronym is at the heart of my rations planning.

For warm weather trips, I calculated the food at 1.4 PPPPD. That's 22.2 ounces of food per person per day. This is considered a shockingly low number by traditional backpackers. But, for my needs (and the needs of a team) with lightweight gear in summertime, it worked out perfectly!

The way to gauge success is to carefully survey how much food is left over at the end of the trip. From my experience, with 1.4 PPPPD there is almost zero.

Even with this seemingly minimal amount of food, everyone on the team eats well. The goal is to be perfectly satisfied during my time in the backcountry but to walk out of the mountains with absolutely ZERO food. It is deeply gratifying to eat that last raisin on the last mile of the last day. If I can do that, the math worked beautifully.

Over the years, I've used this data to refine the food weights for the next trip. Any lower than 1.4 PPPPD and I would run out of food (and I have); any more and I would have had excessive leftovers.

Easy math for the model trip (see tip 12):

1.4 PPPPD × 10 days = 14 pounds of food on Day 1

134. Food weights and glossary

The math here is all done in ounces. With 16 ounces to a pound, conversion gets a little tricky otherwise, unlike that ingenious metric system.

Remember, 0.1 a pound is only 1.6 ounces, less than the weight of a CLIF bar. A Crunchy Peanut Butter CLIF bar weighs 2.4 ounces. This humble bar has 250 calories, which works out to 104 calories per ounce—slightly under our target average of 125 calories per ounce.

- 1.0 ounce = 28.35 grams
- 0.1 pound = 1.6 ounce = 45.5 grams
- 1.4 pounds = 22.4 ounces
- 1 ounce of food = approximately 125 calories
- 0.1 pound of food = approximately 200 calories
- PPPPD = Pounds Per Person Per Day
- PPPD = Per Person Per Day
- Snacks = Non-meals, stuff eaten without a stove.
- Meals = Non-snacks, stuff that (mostly) requires a stove for breakfast or dinner
- Fudge Factor = Avoiding complex (or simple) math when decision making

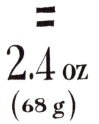

=

2.4 oz

(68 g)

135. Create a food spreadsheet

Your computer can make organizing food data super efficient. I encourage you to formalize the process with a simple

---

spreadsheet program. This rationing format works extremely well, especially if you are planning a long trip with several people.

The data to the right is for ten days of solo camping and is set up to closely match the numbers and items from this food chapter. For a two-person team, just double the amounts. Obviously, everyone has differing food cravings, so feel free to tweak the information presented here. The math should be simple enough that you can easily tailor these ideas to fit your needs.

I *strongly* suggest that if you are planning a trip with a team, do ALL the food math for everyone on ONE spreadsheet. If you attempt to have everyone do their own rationing, expect chaos and a lot of leftover food (trust me on this one).

Factors for the Food Spreadsheet:

- PPPPD
- Number of team members
- Number of days
- Weight of meals per person per day

The calculations will produce:

- Total weight of all food at the start of the trip
- Weight of snacks per day

136. Determine the number of days

How much food is needed for the model trip (see tip 12) of ten days? You won't be eating breakfast out of your rations on Day 1, so don't factor in that first meal. Same at the end; no need for dinner on Day 10, so don't count that meal either. But you *will* eat snack food during the first and last days, so you need to include that as part of the formula.

A ten-day trip is actually nine breakfasts, nine dinners, and ten days of snacks. Let's call this 9.5 days of food. There's no good way to quantify that 0.5 in the equation, so I'm wisely applying the fudge factor. Think of each night spent out as sandwiched between one dinner and one breakfast. Note that some of the charts and figures below will read as ten days, even though the time is really nine nights.

1.4 PPPPD
number of people = 1
number of days = 10
weight of MEALS per person per day = 10 oz

FOOD SPREAD-SHEET

category	#	item	oz
DINNERS	1	couscous/polenta	4.5
	2	couscous/polenta	4.5
	3	rice & beans	4.5
	4	rice & beans	4.5
	5	rice & lentils	4.5
	6	rice & lentils	4.5
	7	pasta	4.5
	8	pasta	4.5
	9	yams (dehydrated)	4.5
		spiced olive oil	5.0
		cheese	4.5
		thai peanut sauce	4.0
		dry pesto powder	2.0
		spice kit	0.6
		spuds as thickener	4.0
B'FASTS	1	oatmeal mix	4.0
	2	oatmeal mix	4.0
	3	oatmeal mix	4.0
	4	oatmeal mix	4.0
	5	spud bomb	4.0
	6	spud bomb	4.0
	7	spud bomb	4.0
	8	two bars	4.0
	9	two bars	4.0
MEAL TOTAL:			**96.6**

SNACKS		gorp (bag a)	16.0
		gorp (bag b)	15.0
		super-spackle	8.0
		home-made GOO	8.0
		groovy-rific bars	16.0
		various bars	16.0
		fritos	16.0
		dried mango	8.0
		salty almonds	8.4
DRINKS		coffee (turkish grind)	8.0
		emergen-C	4.0
		powdered milk	4.0
SNACKS & DRINKS TOTAL:			**127.4**

GRAND TOTAL (ounces)	**224.0**
GRAND TOTAL (pounds)	**14.0**

137. Snacks vs. meals

Snack food is used to define anything that isn't breakfast or dinner; there is no lunch in these calculations. Snacks mean trail food, treats, desserts, goodies, drink mix, and nosh. For clarity in this book, I will only use the term *snacks*.

Meals are defined as breakfast and dinner and any food that will accompany them. Examples include calorie-dense cheese and sauces that are added to a dinner; these weights are added to the "Meals" column.

This ratio should be snack *heavy* and meal *light*. It is easy to spend excessive time creating elaborate dinners in your outdoor kitchen, but be aware that what you'll truly be craving is snacks on the trail. Trust me: The more you have in snacks, the happier you'll be!

Here's a simple follow-up step to your spreadsheet calculations: Before your trip, scrutinize your food again by laying *all* the packaged items out on a big table. Organize the food in tidy piles. Look at every item. Ask yourself, "Do I actually *need* this? Could I replace it with something else? Can I replace any MEAL item with a SNACK item?"

Work with your partners and go through everything. Contemplate your perceived wants and needs. If you review your rations and neither of you likes plain peanuts, don't take 'em. Conversely, if both of you *love* Milky Way bars, add a few more.

CALCULATE THE MEAL WEIGHTS

Don't just guess at the weight of *breakfast* and *dinner* (the meals). There is no need to deal with uneaten leftovers in the backcountry. I feel a very deep responsibility to leave the mountains as clean as I possibly can (see tip 44), and that means I'll be carrying out any leftovers. Tossing them behind a bush (or burying them) simply isn't an option; it's littering. The most efficient strategy is to eat *everything* in your mug at every meal, and that requires precise planning. The weights I'm advocating are an excellent blueprint. Use a scale, weigh it all out, and be diligent with your numbers.

Let's start with 4.5 ounces of dry food (like couscous) per person per dinner. Then add 1.5 ounces of some sort of calorie-dense sauce (or cheese) to this number for a total of 6 ounces per person per dinner. Any more and there might be leftovers; any less and you'll still be hungry. If you're cooking for a team of two, you'll have a 9-ounce bag of

SQUEEZE OUT *all* THE AIR !

DINNER FOR 1 PERSON

dry ingredients for each dinner. Use it all. It can be cooked in a 1-liter pot.

The breakfast number is slightly less, at 4 ounces per person per breakfast. The oatmeal mix and the spud-bomb are the mainstays of my breakfast planning.

1.4 PPPPD = 22.4 oz of food per day	

	4.5 oz dry pasta
	1.5 oz sauce or cheese
(+)	4.0 oz breakfast
(=)	10 oz of meals Per Person Per Day

	22.4 oz total food per day
(−)	10.0 oz weight meals per day
(=)	12.4 oz snacks Per Person Per Day

The math above shows 12.4 ounces of snacks allotted per person per day. Trust this number!

These calculations work well for adults in summer. I've done a lot of fine-tuning over the years with these numbers and big groups, so I feel confident in recommending them. If these numbers don't work for you, simply change the appropriate data points on you spreadsheet to match your needs.

138. How many calories do you need?

Between 2,500 and 3,000 calories PPPD is at the low end, but perfectly adequate for our model trip. Bumping these numbers up is essential when you add more stresses (see tip 140).

A well-balanced ration should average about 125 calories per ounce. This is only an estimate, but it's a tidy number and works nicely for planning (and eating) purposes. Achieving 125 calories per ounce requires creating a rather dense ration plan. This ain't diet food; you are trying to maximize the energy oomph in every ounce.

PPPPD at 125 calories per ounce:

1.4 pounds = 2,800 calories
1.5 pounds = 3,000 calories
1.6 pounds = 3,200 calories
1.7 pounds = 3,400 calories
1.8 pounds = 3,600 calories
1.9 pounds = 3,800 calories
2.0 pounds = 4,000 calories

Food

139. Factors that increase the need for food

WEATHER

Food is fuel. The more energy you expend, the more food you need. One factor that will increase your need for food is cold weather. You can only create internal heat through exercise and metabolism; this requires calories—and that's food! When the temperature goes down, the need for food goes up. Do not take 1.4 PPPPD to the Yukon in December!

EXERTION LEVEL

The physical demands of something like remote mountaineering will require more food. A huge expedition pack loaded with wet ropes and metal hardware will require more energy. When the pack weight goes up, so does the need for food. Himalayan climbers will eat well over 2.5 PPPPD and still lose weight.

DEMANDS OF THE ROUTE

If the proposed route is long and ambitious—such as trying to link the Appalachian, Continental Divide, and Pacific Crest Trails—you'll require more food. Don't try to do multiple 40-mile trail days in a row on 1.4 PPPPD; you'll need *lots* more. When the mileage goes up, so does the need for food per day.

HEIGHTENED BASELINE METABOLISM

If you are a nineteen-year-old guy and the star offensive lineman on your college football team, your metabolic needs are probably different from the rest of the population. You would be well advised to appropriately bump up the numbers and be realistic about the needs of your own body. If you know you need to eat more than the statistical norm, take more. When the healthy hiker eats like a vacuum, the need for food per day goes up.

Is there an exact formula for these inexact problems? Sadly, no. This is where planning, experience, forethought, and the prudent application of the fudge factor come into play.

140. Trip duration influences food needs

On a longer trip, you'll start craving more food. Your body will be adapting, and your metabolism will kick into a higher gear. After about Day 10 on the trail, those PPPPD numbers will need to be bumped up dramatically.

1.4 PPPPD for Days 1 through 10

During the first few days, you might not have much of an appetite. That'll change as you spend time outdoors. You'll recognize an overt ramping-up of your daily needs as you approach Day 10.

1.75 PPPPD for Days 10 through 20

You'll begin to eat more, and you'll be hungry at the end of a long day. Bump up the percentage of fats and protein in the diet. Expect to lose some weight.

2.0 PPPPD for Days 20 through 30 (and Beyond)

Add even more fat and protein. You may feel extremely healthy at this point. Be careful not to eat your own hand during dinner. This is a lot of food for summertime with a light pack. I wouldn't recommend going any higher unless you know your own metabolic needs and foresee cranking out some real-deal mileage.

141. Stuff adds up over time

Going out for a night or two? No big deal if you are a few ounces off in your food prepping. But ten days of food on your back is no joke. The food decisions you make during preplanning will dramatically impact your pack weight.

The difference between 1.4 pounds and 1.6 pounds is a scant 3.2 ounces. Multiply 3.2 by 10 days, and you've got 38.4 ounces, that's almost 2.5 pounds! Or the weight of sixteen CLIF Bars!

A 10-day ration at 1.4 PPPPD = 14 pounds

A 10-day ration at 1.6 PPPPD = 16 pounds

A 10-day ration at 1.8 PPPPD = 18 pounds

A 10-day ration at 2.0 PPPPD = 20 pounds

There is a 6-pound spread noted above for these ten-day ration options—more than the entire base weight of many ultralight backpackers!

142. Balance your food items

- Complex carbohydrates
- Simple carbohydrates
- Protein
- Fat

Prep your diet in the top-down order above. Protein is probably the hardest to include in a long ration, especially for vegetarians. I add some sort of protein bar (the ones used by body builders) as a simple way to supplement my protein needs.

Eat more carbs during the day for ongoing energy on the trail. Eat more fat and protein in the evening, for muscle recovery and warm sleeping. You don't need a doctorate in nutritional sciences to make good choices. If something is sorely lacking (or excessively overloaded), you'll recognize it in the spreadsheet and can fine-tune by applying the nonscientific fudge factor.

143. Bag it all up

Use Ziploc baggies for your food. Make sure to squeeze the air out of each bag, then double-check that the zipper is closed tight. No need to lose food due to a blowout. Write the weight on each bag.

Some plastic bags are lighter than others. This surely qualifies as nerdy (see tip 5), but the weight of packaging will add up on a long trip. There is an aisle in every grocery store that can supply your bagging needs, and the Ziploc style is the lightest option for most of your needs. The same UL rules apply to plastic storage sacks: Take the lightest option available! Those little snack-size baggies are extremely useful for tiny items that need to stay together, such as the repackaged Aquamira (see tip 106).

6½" x 5⅞
0.0081 oz.
each

Evolve sandwich size = 0.081 ounce each—6.5×5.87 inches (15.5×14.9 centimeters)

Snack size = 0.06 ounce each—6.5×3.25 inches—(16.5×8.2 centimeters)

Sandwich size = 0.74 ounce each—6.5× 5.87 inches (15.5×14.9 centimeters)

Storage (quart) = 0.18 ounce each—7×7.75 inches (17.7×19.5 centimeters)

Freezer bag = 0.24 ounce each—7×7.75 inches (17.7×19.5 centimeters)

Freezer bags are made of thicker plastic and thus weigh more. Some folks praise the virtues of freezer bag cooking. This is where you pour boiling water directly into a Ziploc freezer bag with your food and then eat directly from the bag (a long handled spoon is very helpful). I like the concept, but I've found it to be a little messy, especially dealing with the used bags. I can never seem to get 'em clean enough to feel okay about carrying them as trash, especially in bear country (see tip 113).

Another option is the tried-and-true produce bag. These come on a roll in the vegetable aisle and are the absolute lightest option. Ask your friendly grocer if you can grab a few (they'll say yes), and use these larger bags for bigger volume items, such as gorp.

144. Go stove free!
I've done plenty of short trips without a stove, and it can be wonderfully liberating. I make sure to bring a small titanium mug in case I need to build a fire and heat water to help manage an injury or accident. This mug also makes a cute cereal bowl. I deeply enjoy the oatmeal mix (eaten cold) from the breakfast recipes.

The centerpiece of my stoveless diet is a big bag of homemade gorp. I also include dried mango, cheese, a variety of nuts, instant coffee packets, powdered milk, a small loaf of dense pumpernickel bread, Fritos, and chocolate.

If I go stoveless, I bring a mix of powdered milk, protein powder, orange Gatorade, and Emergen-C. I put this in a small 500-milliliter juice bottle, shake vigorously until foamy, and enjoy.

145. What if you run out of food?
If you run out of food, so what? Actually, I think it's a valuable experience. I've run out of food by the end of a trip so many times that I can't keep count anymore. The important lesson I've learned is that it's okay to run out of food. It's a bummer, true enough, but no big deal—just keep hiking!

Maybe I grumble a little more, but it's JUST FINE.

On one occasion in Alaska, my teammates and I all shared the final bits of food on the last afternoon of an eighteen-day expedition. We ate a dinky bag of instant mashed potatoes mixed with raisins and Tabasco, eaten cold (hydrated with glacier runoff, so I mean COLD). Hunger is an amazing thing, 'cuz it was GOOD!

Now if you are planning to do an unsupported traverse of Greenland, you'll want to look closely at the consequences of running out of food, because it could prove disastrous. But if you are hiking a section of the Appalachian Trail in August, you have a less-intense set of variables. Make decisions accordingly.

If you actually do run out of food, here are some strategies for coping: First, *do NOT complain!* This goes for the whole team. It won't help (trust me on this one).

You can expect your pace to drop down a few notches, but not as much as you may think. Also expect to have a difficult time regulating your body heat. You'll get cold a lot quicker, and you'll end up wearing more clothes, even for hiking (a lighter pack!). You'll sleep colder too, so if you have the fuel, make a hot water bottle at bedtime. And make sure to drink plenty of water—no need to add dehydration to your already stressed body.

The biggest issue can be mood; staying upbeat is a challenge. Your ability to stay focused may get clouded by a grumpy mindset. But please know that you can still perform well with the added challenge of no food. The experience can be surprisingly rewarding.

146. Make an insulating cozy

The cozy is just a simple insulator sized to fit the cooking pot. It can be made from some old scraps of sleeping pad foam or from that shiny reflective insulating bubble-wrap stuff. Make one yourself for any size vessel, from the smallest mug to the biggest bucket.

The benefits of the cozy:

- It will easily offset its own weight in fuel savings.
- Some foods will "cook" inside the cozy even when the stove is off.
- It keeps the food warm!
- You can hold the insulated vessel in your hands without burning yourself.
- It makes carrying a pot a little more comfy (the metal doesn't clonk directly into your back).

STANDARD COZY COOKING

Most of the recipes in this book will simply say: *Standard cozy cooking* in the instructions. These meals are all dinners at 4.5 ounces of dry uncooked food per person. The water requirements will all be at 300 milliliters (10 fluid ounces) per person per meal.

One-pot meals require only boiling water. To cook, dump the contents of the bag into the pot (or mug) of boiling water. Then remove the pot from the stove and slip the pot into its form-fitting cozy. Cover it up and let it sit for about five minutes. The cozy does its duty, keeping the hot food insulated and continuing the hydration process. Take off the lid, add approximately 1.5 ounce of some sort of calorie-dense extra goodness, like spiced olive oil. Eat and enjoy!

Some meals require just a little bit of extra cooking (anything with "instant" rice or the angel hair pasta). The instructions will tell you to add more cooking time: This means only about two minutes extra on the stove. For the rice meals, you'll need to avoid burning the bottom of the pan, so you may need to lift the pot off the flame a few extra inches. This requires holding

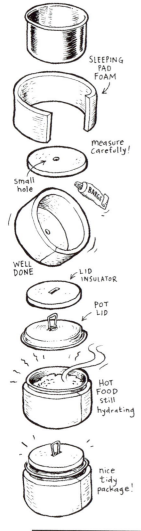

NEAT & TIDY
COZY
CONSTRUCTION

SLEEPING
PAD
FOAM

measure
carefully!

small
hole

BARGE

WELL
DONE

LID
INSULATOR

POT
LID

HOT
FOOD
still
hydrating

nice
tidy
package!

the pot using something other than a gloved hand, like a tiny pot gripper.

147. Groovy-biotic recipes

If you've made a real-deal commitment to going ultralight, you can use that same resolve in your food planning. And you CAN eat very well indeed!

I'm a vegetarian, and I try really hard to eat only organic food. I spent two beautiful weeks in the Big Horns (in central Wyoming) with my pal Lauren, and we are both super-enthusiastic about eating well! This was our chance to really dedicate ourselves to creating a healthy camping diet, all within a UL format. Our rations emphasized whole grains, organic products, and yummy goodness! We worked to minimize dairy or processed sugar.

Lauren and I called our diet *Groovy-Biotic*. That's an accurate nomenclature, if a bit nontechnical! It refers to our selective inclusion of the *grooviest* parts of our vegetarian diet principles in our rations.

Each dinner and breakfast recipe below is made from dry ingredients. Simply dump each of the ingredients into a big bowl, and stir it up. Easy! Then you can bag the individual contents using a scale and Ziploc baggies. Again, easy!

CRUSHED NUT MIX

Take equal portions of almonds, cashews, and sunflower seeds and put them in the food processor; chop until they are fine and granular, but not dust. This mix adds calories and a rich taste to several recipes.

CRUSHED FRITOS (YES, REALLY)

Take Fritos corn chips and put them in the food processor; chop until they are in small chunks. Don't mix them down to dust! Fritos are 160 calories per ounce and add a distinct crunch and corn taste to several recipes.

148. Dinners

RICE AND LENTILS

Standard cozy cooking plus extra stove time.

2 cups instant rice

1½ cups instant lentil soup mix (available in bulk at health food stores)

½ cup crushed nut mix

¼ cup tomato powder

¼ cup golden raisins

¼ cup instant mashed potatoes

¼ cup shredded coconut

1 tablespoon powdered curry

1 teaspoon powdered cumin

1 teaspoon powdered chili powder

½ teaspoon powdered salt

½ teaspoon powdered pepper

½ teaspoon powdered coriander

Dash powdered cardamom

Goes well with the Middle Eastern Tahini Sauce, Thai Peanut Sauce, or Spiced Olive Oil.

RICE AND BEANS

Standard cozy cooking plus extra stove time.

2 cups instant rice

1½ cups instant black bean soup flakes

½ cup crushed nut mix

½ cup crushed Fritos

¼ cup tomato powder

1 tablespoon chili pepper

1 tablespoon dried falafel powder

1 teaspoon cumin

1 teaspoon garlic powder

1 teaspoon oregano

½ teaspoon brown sugar

½ teaspoon powdered salt

½ teaspoon powdered pepper

Goes well with the Spiced Olive Oil and chunks of cheese.

POLENTA-COUSCOUS COMBO

Corn polenta is a product made from corn. Couscous is a Middle Eastern pasta. Both are pretty easy to find in any health food store.

Standard cozy cooking.

2 cups corn polenta

1 cup couscous

¼ cup chopped sun-dried tomatoes

½ cup crushed nut mix

¼ cup pine nuts

¼ cup dried falafel powder

¼ cup tomato powder

1 teaspoon dried basil

½ teaspoon mild paprika

½ teaspoon garlic powder

½ teaspoon onion powder

½ teaspoon each salt and pepper

½ teaspoon dried oregano

Goes well with the Pesto Sauce, Middle Eastern Tahini Sauce, or Spiced Olive Oil.

DEHYDRATED YAMS

This will cause teammates to cry tears of joy. Yams prepared in the dehydrator at home are amazingly wonderful. As a rule, if you start out with 5 pounds of raw yams, you'll end up with 1 pound of dehydrated stuff. I start with organic yams and shred them in my home food processor.

If you put the raw stuff straight into the dehydrator, you'll end up with a product that does *NOT* rehydrate. It ends up the consistency of shoe leather—too chewy to be enjoyed.

You'll need to quickly steam the shredded yams BEFORE they go in the dehydrator. I use a pressure cooker with a tiny bit of water and steam the big load for 1 minute. You can easily use a pot with a vegetable steamer insert. When this mix is later rehydrated, the yams are perfect.

After steaming, fill the dehydrator trays with the mushy orange yam stuff; let it dry overnight. The end product is crumbly stuff with sharp little edges, so I use a thicker plastic bag for storage.

Use standard cozy cooking. Add Thai peanut sauce, and get ready for a teary-eyed culinary event! I've added wild onions to the beautiful yam dish for a little extra pizzazz.

149. The magic of instant mashed potatoes

On any long trip I include a small bag of instant mashed potatoes. This stuff is truly instant; you don't need to cook it at all. If you used too much water and your meal ends up a little runny, you can easily sprinkle some potato flakes in your cup and stir (except oatmeal in the morning). Instantly the runny stuff will get thick and gloppy. And when you're hungry, that extra thickness is more satisfying!

If you are worried about burning your meal (the rice and beans should simmer for a few minutes, and they're easy to burn), it might be a good idea to add a little extra water. This will solve the burning on the bottom of the pot. Adding the instant spuds before serving is a nice trick to absorb that extra water.

There is no need to drain off pasta water; that starchy water is loaded with calories. Simply add the instant spuds to absorb that excess water.

A 5-ounce bag of plain spuds should be fine for a ten-day trip. Approximately 0.5 ounce per person per day is a good way to figure the math.

150. Sauces

Cooked pasta requires flavoring, and hiking long miles requires a boost in calories. The solution is some sort of oil-based spice in a bottle. These sauces have proved themselves to be super successful, creating a dinner that is thoroughly enjoyed—never any leftovers! I make these with extra salt, vinegar, and hot spices to ensure they won't spoil during a long trip in the backcountry.

I factor in 1.5 ounces of sauce per individual meal. That number helps with the math for nine dinners on our model trip. A full bottle (8 fluid ounces/250 milliliters) will weigh about 10 ounces. This will be enough for six one-person meals—about 1.5 ounces of liquid sauce per meal.

Thai Peanut Sauce

2 cups peanut butter

¼ cup apple cider vinegar

¼ cup lime juice

¼ cup soy sauce

¼ cup vegetable oil

4 cloves garlic, crushed

1 tablespoon green curry paste

1 tablespoon brown sugar

2-inch piece fresh ginger, finely chopped

1 cup shredded coconut

1 cup chopped walnuts

¼ cup hot sauce

Combine all ingredients. Add more peanut butter to thicken, more oil to thin.

Middle Eastern Tahini Sauce

2 cups tahini

1 cup olive oil

2 cloves garlic, crushed

½ cup lemon juice

¼ cup falafel powder

1 tablespoon cumin

1 tablespoon salt

½ bunch green onion, finely chopped

1 cup chopped basil or cilantro

¼ cup chopped sunflower seeds

⅓ cup vinegar

⅓ cup soy sauce

Combine all ingredients. Add more tahini to thicken, more olive oil to thin.

Pesto

2 cups olive oil

1 cup shredded Parmesan cheese

½ cup shredded Romano cheese

3 cups chopped fresh basil

¼ cup crushed garlic

½ cup chopped sun-dried tomatoes

1 cup chopped walnuts

½ cup pine nuts

1 tablespoon salt

½ tablespoon pepper

½ cup lemon juice

¼ cup vinegar

¼ cup dry Italian spice

Combine all ingredients. Add more Parmesan to thicken, more olive oil to thin.

POWDERED PESTO SAUCE

You can easily create a dried pesto mix in your kitchen. All the ingredients are easy to find in any grocery store. This can be added to angel hair pasta with the Spiced Olive Oil. Approximate requirements: 2 ounces per person per ten-day ration.

½ cup dried or granular Parmesan cheese

½ cup chopped nut mix

¼ cup powdered milk

1 heaping tablespoon garlic powder

1 heaping tablespoon basil powder

1 teaspoon oregano

1 teaspoon sugar

1 teaspoon pepper

1 teaspoon sugar

Combine all ingredients and stir.

SPICED OLIVE OIL

You can easily create a big batch of all the ingredients below for an intensely satisfying universal flavor bomb.

4 cups olive oil

½ cup garlic cloves (this'll liquefy in the blender)

¼ cup basil powder

¼ cup oregano powder

1 teaspoon mild red paprika

½ teaspoon salt

½ teaspoon pepper

Combine all ingredients in a blender and process until the mixture is nice and smooth. I stored the goodness in a 250-milliliter water bottle lifted from an airplane ride.

Approximately 250 milliliters per person per ten-day ration is a good target amount, but more would get eaten!

BOTTLES FOR OILS AND SAUCES

Little Nalgene bottles are easy to find at most outdoor shops. But these are heavy, decidedly *not* UL!

The humble 500-milliliter plastic water bottle from any grocery store or gas station meets the UL requirements (0.6 ounce). These are pretty close to foolproof, but not quite. If the bottles are loaded with anything oily, pack them in a redundant plastic bag. A leaky bottle of oil would be disastrous, especially in bear country.

The 500-milliliter Platypus (0.8 ounce) is the crème de la crème of liquid sauce storage.

THE UL SPICE KIT

Packaged in teenie-weenie plastic bags, 1 teaspoon per bag. Weight: less than 1 ounce.

- Salt
- Pepper
- Tony Chachere's Original Creole Seasoning (a highly recommended spicy pepper mix found in most grocery stores)
- Chipotle powder or cayenne pepper (hot!)

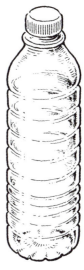

500 ml
CHEAPO
WATER BOTTLE
0.6 OZ

THE UL SPICE KIT
weighs less than 1 ounce!

151. Breakfasts

OATMEAL OR SPELT FLAKES

Don't underestimate oatmeal as a source of protein. One-half cup of cooked oatmeal has 6 grams of protein; an egg has 7 grams. The egg is a complete protein; the oats require some other amino acids to be a complete protein, which can be achieved by adding nuts and fruit to the oatmeal mix. Spelt flakes (a wheat product available at health food stores) are an alternative to traditional rolled oats. Spelt has a higher protein count, cooks much quicker, and is less chewy when eaten cold.

Some folks need more variety, but I can eat this mix every morning. It can be made with cold water (nice while on the trail!) or hot on a chilly morning.

2 cups spelt flakes (or rolled oats)

2 cups crushed nut mix

½ cup powdered milk

¼ cup dried cranberries

¼ cup protein powder

1 teaspoon vanilla extract

1 teaspoon almond extract

Pinch salt

Dash cinnamon

Goes well with Super-Spackle.

MASHED POTATOES FOR BREAKFAST

Make it right in your mug; just add hot water. Lovingly called the Spud-Bomb.

2 cups instant mashed potatoes

½ cup crushed nut mix

¼ cup tomato powder

½ cup crushed Fritos

¼ cup chopped sun-dried tomatoes

¼ cup dried falafel powder

¼ cup shredded Parmesan cheese

½ teaspoon garlic powder

½ teaspoon onion powder

½ teaspoon each salt and pepper

½ teaspoon dried oregano

Goes well with Spiced Olive Oil.

JUST EAT A FEW BARS FOR BREAKFAST

Wanna get a really quick start in the morning? Simply roll out of bed and choke down some gorp or a couple of bars. No need to fire up a stove or even use a spoon. This no-brainer technique will dramatically simplify the morning.

If you decide to forgo a cooked breakfast, make sure to plan ahead so that you aren't pilfering from your precious "Snack" column. Add the weight of these bars into the "Meal" column when you prepare your spreadsheet.

152. Snacks

GORP (GOOD OL' RAISINS & PEANUTS)

This is at the heart of my snacking. Practically every backpacker starts a hike with a bag full of dried fruit and nuts. I do not buy pre-made gorp; I make my own. I figure I'm smart enough to make exactly what I truly want. My mainstay is a combo of cashews, walnuts, golden raisins, dark chocolate chips, cranberries, and a pinch of salt—that's all. I've never found another combo more satisfying.

IN PRAISE OF FRITOS

The most efficient ultralight food would be the highest calories for the lowest weight.

The ingredients in original Fritos are corn, corn oil, and salt—that's all. That adds up to 160 calories per ounce: 10 grams of fat, 2 grams of protein, and 170 milligrams of sodium. I am NOT trying to call Fritos a health food, but I do say they pack a caloric wallop. Save a little bit of space in the pack by precrunching them, at least a little bit.

Pringles? These are the beloved snack of the ultralight enthusiast. I don't understand why—Fritos supplies 6.25 percent more calories per ounce!

HOMEMADE GOO

I've concocted homemade sports gel in my kitchen, and it has been wildly successful! I read the ingredient of a few popular endurance gel products, and I thought, *Geesh, this stuff is simple!*

2 cups brown rice syrup; available at health food stores (carbs)

¼ cup cashew butter (fat)

¼ cup protein powder; vanilla seems to work best (protein)

Pinch salt (electrolyte)

Maybe a dash of hot water to thin it down

Recipes

I make this stuff in a blender. Warm the brown rice syrup for at least half an hour by placing the jars in a tub (or the sink) with very hot water. Don't use a microwave, which will create bad vibes. The syrup needs to be thin enough that you don't burn out the motor in your blender.

Pour the syrup into the blender, and have some very hot water ready for adding to the syrup. A little is all you'll need to thin it out.

Slowly add cashew butter and protein powder. That's it!

When I do a long trip, I carry the goo in a 500-milliliter Platypus. I use a funnel and fill up the vessel while the mixture is still warm and runny. For short trips I use a plastic marathon runner's gel flask, available at any endurance sport store.

SUPER-SPACKLE

This stuff is so ridiculously rich that just a tiny bit is unbelievably gratifying. Initially I wanted to create something calorie packed that I could add to my morning oatmeal, but I found that this stuff is way better straight from the bottle. I package it in a 500-milliliter Platypus and use it like a squeeze tube so I can partake of its goodness without a spoon. Any time Super-Spackle comes out of my backpack, I find myself surrounded by very friendly teammates with their spoons at the ready! Use 500 milliliters per person per ten days as a tidy volume for your spreadsheet.

SUPER SPACKLE

500 ml PLATYPUS

1 cup almond butter

1 cup cashew butter

½ cup agave syrup

¼ cup almond oil

1 tablespoon vanilla extract

1 teaspoon almond extract

Pinch salt

Start by putting the jars and bottles in a tub of very hot water; let them warm up for at least half an hour. This makes the mixing process a lot easier.

Combine all the ingredients in a big sturdy bowl. With a fork and a strong arm, start mixing it all together. This stuff is gloppy and thick. Get it just thin enough that you can get it through a funnel and into your vessel. You can add a little more of the almond oil if the mixture's too thick.

If you don't have a Platypus, use a 500-milliliter plastic bottle. The kind they sell at the grocery store for spring water works really well. The plastic is just a little thinner than a standard soda bottle and makes a good *squeeze* bottle.

HOMEMADE NO-BAKE GROOVY-RIFIC BARS

A calorie dense alternative to expensive store-bought bars. Easy to make and delicious.

1 cup almonds

1 cup cashews

1 cup walnuts

2 cups spelt flakes (or rolled oats)

½ cup golden raisins

½ cup dried cranberries

½ cup coconut oil

½ cup brown rice syrup

½ cup almond butter

1 cup finely chopped dates

1 tablespoon vanilla extract

1 tablespoon hazelnut (or almond) extract

½ cup tapioca flour

1 teaspoon salt

Combine almonds, cashews, walnuts, and spelt flakes (or oats) in a food processor. Pulse briefly, until the mix is granular with

minimal chunks. Place this mixture in a big mixing bowl. Add the raisins and cranberries.

In a small saucepan, heat coconut oil over very low heat. Add brown rice syrup and almond butter. Stir until the mixture is a smooth consistency; add the chopped dates. Remove saucepan from heat and add vanilla and hazelnut (or almond) extracts into this mixture.

Add the oily mixture into the large mixing bowl and stir the contents with a wooden spoon until completely mixed. Add the tapioca flour and salt, and continue mixing with your hands.

Press this mixture into glass baking dishes or cake pans. Chill in the refrigerator for 1 hour, until mixture hardens.

Remove from refrigerator, and cut into bars or squares.

Put a small amount of tapioca flour in a large plastic bag. Put the squares in the bag with the flour and gently shake. This creates a dusty covering to keep the bars from being too oily or sticky.

153. Ultralight skills can simplify the rest of your life

Camping in the wilderness has changed me. I look back at the person I was before I began taking part in bold expeditions into the mountains, and it seems everything about me has changed. Ultralight camping has changed me even more. I go into the wilderness for my metaphysical fix, as a renewal of spirit. Obviously I can't live the entirety of my life out there in *that* world, but I can bring something back with me and try to integrate it with the challenges of *this* world.

The simplicity and ease of camping and traveling with minimal gear is a precious life lesson. The value might be hard to articulate, but it is most assuredly very real. I lead a very simple life, and the things I once thought were important have faded away, leaving just a core of beautiful essentials.

I wish I could spell it out in a few witty sentences and illustrate it with a quirky cartoon, but I can't. The lessons are too subtle and, at the same time, profound. Maybe, between the lines of this book and hidden in the drawings, you'll find some tiny clues that will point you to a simpler life philosophy. This is really the ultimate tip, because if you pay attention, you'll find that ultralight camping means a more rewarding awareness, not only in the wilderness but also in your everyday life.

Peace,

Mike C!

Suggested reading

Jardine, Ray. *Trail Life: Ray Jardine's Lightweight Backpacking*. AdventureLore Press, 2009.

Jordan, Ryan. *Lightweight Backpacking and Camping: A Field Guide to Wilderness Equipment, Technique, and Style*. Beartooth Mountain Press, 2005.

Ladigin, Don, and Mike Clelland (illustrator). *Lighten Up! A Complete Handbook for Light and Ultralight Backpacking*. FalconGuides, 2005.

O'Bannon, Allen, and Mike Clelland (illustrator). *Allen & Mike's Really Cool Backpackin' Book: Traveling & Camping Skills for a Wilderness Environment*. Falcon-Guides, 2001.

Sailer, Dave. *Fire in Your Hand: Dave's Little Guide to Ultralight Backpacking Stoves*. CreateSpace, 2008.

Resources

This book has a nifty companion website! The online counterpart will be a way to share new advice, gear reviews, and additional information about ultralight backpackin' and all its quirky nuances. And, if you have any cool tips, please lemme know!

www.ultralightbackpackintips.blogspot.com

www.antigravitygear.com

www.backpackinglight.com

www.golite.com

www.gossamergear.com

www.traildesigns.com

www.zpacks.com

About the Author

Mike Clelland! never went to art school, studying *Mad Magazine* instead. Mike grew up in the flat plains of Michigan, then spent ten years (as a yuppie!) in New York City. In 1987 he thought it might be fun to be a ski bum in Wyoming for the winter. Unfortunately, after living and skiing in the Rockies, he found it quite impossible to return to his previous life in the Big City. Mike is presently living in a shed in Idaho where he divides his time between illustrator and NOLS instructor.